Praise for *Patio* and Jamie Durie

' *Patio* is the kind of publication you pick up when you're lamenting your daggy backyard with its dirty old back steps and tired old fence. It leads you into a world of beautiful backyards, where water trickles down artfully constructed walls and boundaries are painted in funky shades...'
SYDNEY WEEKLY

' Advice appears in many forms, but one of the freshest voices comes from Jamie Durie...'
USA TODAY

' *Patio* is eye candy for voyeurs with some stunning Sydney courtyards, while also delivering a well-sourced stock of garden ideas...a bit like Durie himself!'
AUSTRALIAN HOUSE AND GARDEN

' [Durie's work] is consistently contemporary, without being overly trendy, featuring beautiful and inviting outdoor living spaces, rather than ornamental showpieces.'
CANADIAN INTERIORS

' The ultimate in coffee-table books...'
HERALD SUN

' ...a gorgeous exploration of Australian gardens...'
AUSTRALIAN WOMEN'S WEEKLY

' ...even if gardening's not your thing, this is a lovely book to plant on the coffee table.'
NEW ZEALAND HOUSE & GARDEN

' [*Patio* has] acres – or corners – of garden inspiration...'
VOGUE LIVING

' With beautiful images, design ideas and handy tips for the home renovator, *Patio* will inspire you to pull on the garden gloves and perform your own *Backyard Blitz*.'
GEELONG TIMES

' The talents of this celebrity gardener are simply divine. They include planning, design and use of unusual materials including sensational water features and mood lighting. From grand scale gardens to small balconies and entertainment areas to lush swimming pools – you'll love them all.'
AUSTRALIAN WINE SELECTOR

JAMIE DURIE
PATIO
GARDEN DESIGN & INSPIRATION

Photography by David Matheson

A Sue Hines Book
ALLEN & UNWIN

This paperback edition published 2006
First published in 2002

A Sue Hines Book
Allen & Unwin
83 Alexander Street
Crows Nest NSW 2065
Australia

Phone: (61 2) 8425 0100
Fax: (61 2) 9906 2218
Email: info@allenandunwin.com
Web: www.allenandunwin.com

National Library of Australia
Cataloguing-in-Publication entry:
Durie, Jamie.

            Patio : garden design & inspiration.
            ISBN 978 1 74114 654 7 (pbk.).
            1. Gardens - Design. 2. Landscape gardening. I. Title.

            712.2

Designed and typeset by MAU Design
Printed in China through Colorcraft Ltd., Hong Kong

10 9 8 7 6 5 4 3

CONTENTS

Introduction

For as long as I can remember I've loved the outdoors. Throughout my childhood I swam, surfed, water-skied, went camping and hiking, built cubby houses, dams and even the odd go-cart, but I never imagined I would end up designing gardens.

How did I get here? Well, it's a long story, but I can tell you I started travelling at the age of 18 and over a period of 10 years I was constantly on the move, visiting places like South Africa, Hong Kong, North America, New Zealand, Taiwan and just about every country in Europe. All the while I was like an insatiable sponge absorbing the art, architecture and lifestyles of the many different cultures I encountered.

Then the travel became tedious and I started to yearn for a place where I could dig my feet in and find an occupation that would keep me creatively satisfied. I met some remarkable designers in Europe and our very own Paul Bangay here in Australia and decided to try my hand at garden design.

There was just one small problem: I was hopeless at keeping plants alive. Truly, I was an expert at killing them, and my mother, a keen gardener, will confirm it was an area I needed to work on. So I put my suitcase into storage and started a full-time course at Ryde Horticultural College in Sydney, emerging three years later with a Diploma of Horticulture in Landscape Design. I established a quaint little garden shop and collected all the bits and pieces that expressed my style. Out the back I set up an old drawing board for the occasional design commission and the shop paid the rent. Three years later the design side of the business had exploded and we had to move to larger premises. My staff had quad-rupled and commissions were coming in from all over the world. Patio, the business, was born.

These days I don't give tips only to Mum on how to keep the garden alive but also to a couple of million viewers every Sunday night courtesy of the TV show *Backyard Blitz* produced by garden guru Don Burke for the Australian Nine Network. I love doing the show and, of course, life changed dramatically for me once I became a TV face, but a lot of people don't realise that my work at Patio continues and the business is going from strength to strength.

First and foremost, I'm a garden designer and this is what *Patio* is all about. It's a visual record of my creative preoccupations: in 'Here and Now' I look at gardens that are typical of the contemporary Australian style; in 'Water' I look at water features, pools and working with the environment; 'People' explores another of my obsessions – making a garden people-friendly and set up for living outdoors; and in 'Places' you'll see the cultural influences – particularly from the East – that affect my work. This book also reflects the development of my work practices over the last four years. The gardens you see here were chosen to reflect the wide variety of commissions we carry out and the unusual challenges we are presented with.

I hope you'll find a lot of ideas in here that inspire you. To help you along, I've provided Design Keys for several of the gardens. These lists of materials and plants will help all you do-it-yourselfers to take the next step and use them in your own outdoor space. I've also thrown in a bit of extra info, listing my all-time favourite plants and giving you a peek at a personal obsession – my beloved cactus collection.

But before we see the results of the designs, let's go back to the very start when it's just me and the clients and the garden-to-be.

In the Beginning

For me a garden is a place to relax with friends and family as well as being a refuge where you can take time out of your busy day for some solitary recharging. The first thing I consider when I meet the clients and see the site is how I would arrange their garden if it were mine. Then I do my best to get to know the owners, asking them loads of questions about their lifestyle and the choices they have made inside and outside the house. More often than not, it's the small things that matter most: it could be a piece of furniture, a work of art, even the fabric on their cushions, but this attention to detail provides vital clues.

I have never championed a particular style of garden. I let the inspiration from the brief, the site and the owners dictate the result because only then, I believe, does the design succeed. There's no doubt a firm hand is needed to guide the clients through a concept, but a designer must never forget the importance of client involvement in the creative journey.

To give you an idea of the process I go through, these are some of the things I focus on when I begin a job:

SUNLIGHT

Find out where the sunniest areas are in the garden. This is not only for the benefit of plants but for people. There's nothing more magnetic than a spot showered with morning light, and good garden design is all about arranging subtle magnets to draw us outside.

PRIVACY

Large or small, every garden needs an element of privacy, intimacy and security. I'm always searching for ways to screen unsightly outlooks and for places to instal partitions that also serve as 'backdrops' for attractive features.

BEST VIEWPOINTS

Ascertaining the best viewpoints from the house is a must. I pay special attention to these vistas, framed by a window or an open door. As long as they don't look contrived they can be wonderful compositions in themselves and yet blend perfectly into the garden when viewed from outside.

NUTS AND BOLTS

Then there is the practical and functional side: check soils for their mineral content, take care of drainage, provide for children and animals, consider access and utilities, shelter vehicles and, of course, establish entertainment areas.

Once I or one of my team have met the clients and as much information as possible has been gathered, it's time to transfer all of the on-site inspirations and ideas to paper and hard drive. I find it very easy to get my ideas across verbally but when it comes to presenting it on paper, well let's just say it's not my greatest strength. Fortunately for me, this is where my design family – the Patio team – really shines. They are a terrific group of highly skilled and talented young designers, horticulturalists, draftspeople and architects and I'm so lucky to have found them. As soon as the job's in, everyone goes to work bringing their experience and expertise to the planning and production process. Many elements need to be taken into account when executing a design, such as site levels, soils and drainage, lighting, irrigation, council by-laws, water feature mechanics, structural engineering, colours, textures, materials and of course plant choice. A huge amount of organisation goes on before the first spade bites the dirt, then it can take anything from a single afternoon to several months to get the job done, depending on the size of the project.

Every garden is different, every client is different and I've got stories about both that would make your hair curl, but the end result has always been worth it. I gain immense fulfilment from my work and great satisfaction when I see the look on the face of a happy client.

1
HERE AND NOW

Here and Now

Whenever I'm away from home I hear people raving about the vast beauty of Australia, the gloriously temperate climate and our diverse multicultural society with its wonderful influences. What I love most about this country is the willingness of people from all walks of life to take on board new ideas and concepts. It's amazing how traditionalists will shift their point of view, and immensely satisfying to pitch a new concept to a conservative client and have the idea embraced with enthusiasm.

My job is a whole lot more than just selecting the right plants, and I'm constantly on the lookout for new materials and visual 'triggers'. Inspiration can be found in seemingly the most mundane things: a crack in a wall, the curve of a fence-post or the serration of a leaf. I drive people crazy with my terrible habit of tuning out of a conversation mid-sentence because something has caught my eye and I'm storing it away for future reference.

Choosing the right building materials is one of the most crucial parts of the process. Glass, copper, steel, resins and plastic are interesting substitutes for concrete, stone, clay and terracotta. Copper is a fantastic metal to work with, and the swirling green patina that builds up on the surface as the metal oxidises lends a contemporary piece a sense of age and history.

The visual relationship between a manu-factured material and a natural free-form plant is fascinating, and you'll see a lot of it in my work.

Place these 'odd' partners side by side and suddenly you have an intangible sense of balance: think of multiple rows of lavender planted out in troughs made of glass, or clumps of native grasses in a stainless steel tub, or rambling ground covers spilling from copper shutters attached to a vertical wall. I get the same buzz when I see water drifting over slabs of glass back-lit with fibre-optic light. For me, this is just another interpretation of what occurs in a natural riverbed when the sun catches water moving over pebbles.

Contemporary garden design is about bending the rules, trying alternative plant choices and combinations and experimenting with old and new materials. When I was studying horticulture, I used to come up with bizarre plant combinations for our mock-up designs. Coupling lavender with agaves, for example, was the kind of thing that used to horrify my teachers but in a strange way I think their resistance helped create the monster.

These days whenever I have a couple of hours to kill, you'll find me poking about an abandoned factory or industrial site searching for odd bits and pieces to make the next garden unique. My friends call it my 'weird fetish', I say it's just doing my bit for recycling. There's a world of everyday objects (probably some gathering dust in your back shed right now) that would be perfect for a neglected spot in your garden or as a container for a new plant. So go on...have some fun with it!

'Floating Landscape' : an interior garden
commissioned by Herman Miller Furniture

LIVINGROOM IN THE SUN

A busy lawyer couple with a baby on the way came to me with a challenge. Their city terrace had an ugly internal courtyard wedged between the diningroom/kitchen and outdoor office. There was no scope to move, and they had little privacy as neighbours could peer into the courtyard from above. Most of all, they were heartily sick of staring at a hot, bland concrete 'box'.

A water feature would instantly cool the area and since there was a shortage of space it made sense to go for a vertical structure. One of my goals is to ensure that the features and focal points I build can be viewed from every possible window and doorway in the house so the position of the water feature in the courtyard had to be exact. Positioned on the western wall, the feature would avoid excess evaporation and catch the morning sun at breakfast time. It was designed so that the future toddler could safely play with the water running down the wall but she wouldn't be able to get at the reservoir below due to the large custom-built galvanised grill camouflaged by a mound of granite pebbles.

Brick-rendered benches run along the side walls, with the hard surfaces softened by cushions and bolsters. The client and my clever stylist friend, Nadine, helped find the perfect fabric from the Designers Guild to provide a very personal touch. It's important to have this kind of input from the owner as the garden progresses. The creation should be a joint experience; I'm just the tour guide.

A product called Natureed provides much-needed screening. It clads the fences and is used as a shade to filter light. The large-format paving is a tranquil green colour: any darker and it would be too hot on little feet as well as shrinking the space; any lighter would be too bright with the sun reflecting off it all day. Around the paving a trench of flat chocolate pebbles gives the floor a floating feeling. (I made double-sure they were all over 50 mm so the new baby couldn't swallow them.)

A tall growth of black bamboo *(Phyllostachys nigra)* flanking the western bench shields the afternoon sun. Galvanised planters containing a row of Australian native grass called *Lomandra longifolia* are bolted along the top of the fenceline. More galvanised planters are tucked under the stairs on the opposite side of the garden and filled with agaves and a row of liriope (also known as lily turf). The wall facing the kitchen is painted a deep, rich magenta with a series of stainless steel cables strung out from the planter at its base to allow a healthy star jasmine to creep almost four metres up the warm bricks.

The main garden is bathed in sun for about three-quarters of the day and is planted out with cycads, some smaller Arizona cacti, golden barrel cactus and a tall, furry *Cleistocactus,* which I call cat's tails.

*The Natureed screen filters
light and provides privacy.*

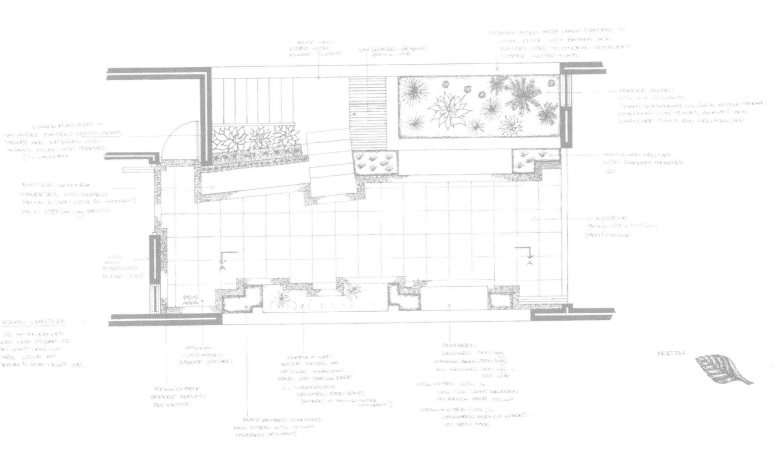

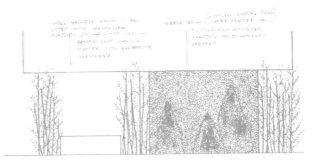

IT'S IMPORTANT TO HAVE THIS KIND OF INPUT FROM THE OWNER AS THE GARDEN PROGRESSES. THE CREATION SHOULD BE A JOINT EXPERIENCE; I'M JUST THE TOUR GUIDE.

Comfortable, elegant and user-friendly, this internal courtyard has been carefully child-proofed.

DESIGN KEY

The custom-made planter boxes are 200 mm x 200 mm x 800 mm galvanised steel with a safety edge.

Pebbles in the water feature are 20-30 mm white 'arctic' quartz pebbles, fixed to the wall with tile adhesive and grout.

Walls are clad with 1.8 m Natureed (this comes in 3.6 m rolls), tied off with galvanised wire.

Spike spotlights used through the garden are 20 watts. Pillar lights and submersible lights for use in the water feature are 50 watts.

Fabric from Designers Guild is cotton acrylic mix, double scotch-guarded with a sponge interior.

Boncote 'library red' limewash

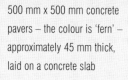

500 mm x 500 mm concrete pavers – the colour is 'fern' – approximately 45 mm thick, laid on a concrete slab

Pebbles around the paving are loose 50-70 mm chocolate 'bracken' pebbles mixed with 50-75 mm 'arctic' quartz. These pebbles should be available from your local landscape supplier.

'Eucalyptus green' limewash

'Bluecow' limewash

Plants

STONE WALL

It's great when your clients are as adventurous as you are. The outgoing couple who own this split-level warehouse-style apartment enjoy their privacy but wanted to spend more of their leisure time outside.

A large brick wall that dominated the view from the livingroom was the first challenge. We decided to turn it into a feature incorporating the energy and movement of running water. The wall is close to the livingroom so, to avoid intrusive noise, the water would have to run down a textured face avoiding a free-fall splash. The polished stainless steel surface of the water wall would have been uncomfortably dazzling on the eyes, so I experimented with some test sheets to find a solution. By trial and error, I discovered the more subtle process of beadblasting achieved the same matt effect as sandblasting without warping the metal.

The main building structure is dominated by hard lines so using organic shapes to interrupt the passage of water would provide an interesting contrast. We settled on large river stones sliced in half with a diamond blade and chose the largest variety of natural colours available with the idea of recapturing the superb hues of the Australian landscape. After a lot of messing about we discovered the perfect angle to spray the water onto the sheet of steel so that it was evenly distributed without any drips or surges of white water. The polished stainless steel architrave was also retained to replicate a picture frame.

A small planter sunk into the pond holds a spray of black bamboo that conceals the dramatic change of height in the wall. The timber seats are constructed from western red cedar and Tasmanian oak. (Many hours were spent in the studio experimenting with the best-shaped lumber support for the benches.) The seats are one of the most beautiful features of the garden and are lovingly waxed on a regular basis to maintain their matt finish.

At one end of the garden a spiral staircase leads to the upstairs balcony. A 270-degree circular galvanised planter follows the curve of the stairs. The pie-shaped pieces of the planter rise with the stairs and, to emphasise the line, the plants also increase in height starting with mini mondo grass then standard mondo grass up to liriope to dietes and finally lomandra. Bursts of agaves decorate the eastern wall and, on the upstairs balcony, three white glazed pots contain magnificent specimens of *Draceana draco*.

At night, low voltage halogens discreetly pick up the corrugations in the steel, the stems of black bamboo and the shimmer of droplets breaking the surface tension of the pond.

AT NIGHT, LOW VOLTAGE
HALOGENS DISCREETLY PICK UP
THE CORRUGATIONS IN THE STEEL,
THE STEMS OF BLACK BAMBOO
AND THE SHIMMER OF DROPLETS
BREAKING THE SURFACE TENSION.

*The upstairs balcony features
three magnificant dragon trees.*

INSTALLATION ART

One of four large warehouse conversions with lots of space and light, this apartment had a two-storey glassed-in garden nestled in a challenging space between the kitchen and livingroom. In addition to plants and seating, the owners wanted a sculptural installation that could be seen from as many viewpoints in the house as possible.

Working with the principle that narrow, vertical stripes can make people look slimmer, it followed that introducing narrow, vertical 'strips' would make the space soar. Several sketch pads later and we had the image of a series of large-format timber beams of varying lengths, fixed carefully in random positions.

These beams were a great find. Having unearthed them from the base of a huge stack of reject timber in a recycling yard, I was told they'd been originally salvaged from an old bridge. After planing back the dirty grey exterior, we discovered the timber was tallow wood – a rather expensive and sought-after material that is almost impossible to get hold of these days. It was very satisfying being able to resurrect a discarded piece of history with the bonus of using recycled material.

Three of the beams are clad with copper so that water can drizzle down their length into a stainless steel reservoir below. Not surprisingly given its former life, this timber is ideal for wet areas so the water-run is no problem at all.

The velvety chocolate limewash as background colour absorbs reflective light while its lush depths enliven the solid timber beams. The difficult ledge on the western wall is concealed so the wall appears as a single plane.

A couple of *Strelitzia nicolai* provide height, and dwarf burgundy cordylines and *Liriope muscari* fringe the benches. At night, fingers of light beam through wooden slats beneath the benches forming slender patterns on the cool charcoal tiles.

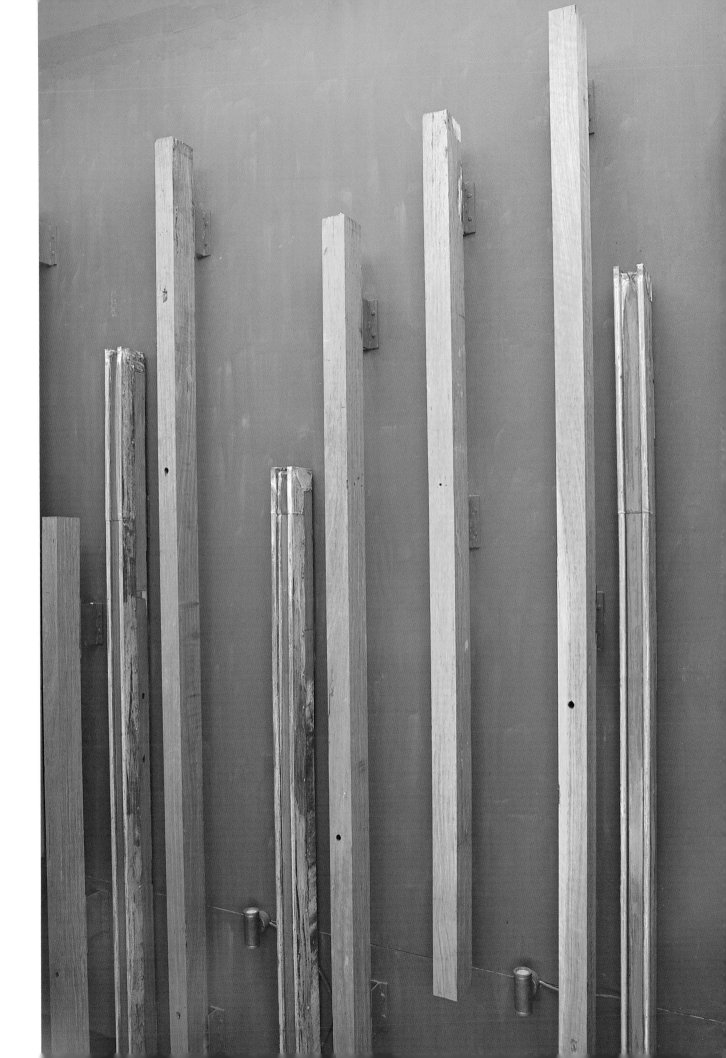

THE VELVETY CHOCOLATE
LIMEWASH ABSORBS REFLECTIVE
LIGHT WHILE ITS LUSH DEPTHS
ENLIVEN THE SOLID TIMBER BEAMS.

QUINTESSENTIALLY AUSTRALIAN

A garden show installation, this is a multi-layered yet minimalist garden, ideal for privacy, relaxation and entertaining. It is also distinctly antipodean, reflecting a number of elements that I think of as quintessentially Australian in its choice of plant species and colour palette, and in catering for our appetite for outdoor living, day or night.

In my mind, there's nothing more Australian than a verandah, patio or deck made of native timber. Here the soft wood provides an interesting contrast to the industrial steel – both stainless steel and rusted – of the walls. These rendered walls are painted a rust shade with iron filings in the mix. The palette was determined primarily by natural processes. Rust reminds us of the red earth and our rural and manufacturing origins; eucalypt leaves reflect the copper hues; red-tipped new foliage is typical of native plant species such as lilly-pilly; and in the water feature, slabs of frosted resin capture the dominant blues and greens of our sea and sky. Another rich colour element is provided by black sand, an industrial by-product.

More and more Australians are embracing the benefits of using native plants. Natives attract birds, have generally lower water requirements and are well suited to surviving our harsh and varied environmental conditions. The plants here reflect aspects of our culture, whether they be the gnarled and hardy serrated-leaf banksia, or the delicate ornamental ground covers that spill out of copper troughs into the pond. The *Leucodendron* cultivar is a fine example of adaptation: originally from South Africa it has been developed and improved in Australian nurseries and is now thoroughly attuned to our climate and conditions.

The variety of plant heights echoes the changes of level in the decking, and key viewpoints are elevated to create delightful new perspectives of the garden's elements. The copper planters and Corten trough planters fixed to the wall are custom made. (Corten is a steel product designed to rust only to a certain point, resulting in a clean, stylised industrial look.)

For many of us, our working days are so busy that we only get to enjoy our gardens when we come home in the evening. This is just one of many reasons why good lighting is essential to reap the full benefit of a contemporary Australian garden. In this display, copper wall-mounted spots light the entranceway. The water feature is up-lit with two fibre-optic cables, with lines of directed light and washes of ambient light glow to illuminate the frosted resin panels and pick up the play of water tumbling over the arrises.

Inspired by the strong, unsymmetrical yet perfectly balanced works of the great American architect, Frank Lloyd Wright, the water feature is made up of frosted resin slabs overlapping each other to create an uneven horizontal stack. Water enters from all three sides of the deck and spills over the reflective pond, which acts as a binding force, linking each end of the garden and all the elements in between.

DESIGN KEY

23 mm frosted resin panels are custom-made. Dry-stacked and placed carefully to achieve maximum water movement, they double as stepping stones over the pond.

For a subtle lighting effect, all lights are 12 volts, either 20 watts, or 50 watts for trees and accents. We have used copper wall spotlights and step lights in the fascia of the seating. The lights used in the pond have a rubber seal.

The walls are painted with a rust shade that contains iron filings in the mix. We used 'liquid iron' followed by a coat of 'instant rust'.

Benches, decking and surfaces are 90 mm x 19 mm treated pine decking with mahogany stain.

The pond is sealed with Beautyliner — a rubber-based, 1 mm membrane — on a timber frame.

Mulch in planters is from recycled crushed glass. Don't use your own bottles for this: go to suppliers who meet ASA standards where the product is crushed and rolled so edges won't cut.

Custom-made Corten trough planters fixed to the wall. The Corten steel is aged with the acid compound 'liquid metal'.

Custom-made copper planters with patina created with the acid compound 'patina green'.

Black sand is used as mulch.

Plants

1 Coast Banksia *Banksia integrifolia*
2 Fan Flower *Scaevola* sp.
3 Grevillea *Grevillea* sp.
4 Leucodendron *Leucodendron* sp.

SKY GARDEN

Often an outdoor living space is neglected because it simply lacks the right elements to entice people to use it. This sunny rooftop garden had a perfectly decent barbecue built into the eastern side of the deck but there was nowhere to sit. The clients enjoyed entertaining and with summer coming they were hoping to treat their guests to some rooftop dining so their request was pretty straightforward: make the garden more user-friendly and attractive.

Early on, I discovered they loved their stainless steel kitchen so I began to look for ways to work the metal into the design. A water feature was another of their requests although, as is usually the case in these urban areas, space was limited. The solution was a long, narrow and very streamlined water feature constructed entirely from stainless steel except for the thin moon-shaped copper bowl where the source originates. Water spills from the bowl into the trough, which slowly fills and overflows evenly across the lip into the main trough below.

My one big mistake was not measuring the stairwell first. It turns out the main pond was so long and heavy that it was impossible to bring up the stairs. I thought a helicopter might strain the budget a little so I called up a few buddies and we all went over the rooftop and heaved it up four stories with some long sturdy ropes and a lot of whingeing. That afternoon cost me quite a few beers!

Either side of the trough are flip-up benches with stainless steel surrounds and flip-out legs. Galvanised iron planters hold two very healthy *Agave attentuata* with a 75 mm granite pebble as a mulch. In the pond a raft of white arum lillies *(Zantedeschia aethiopica)* float lazily in the sun.

The final touch is a large dining table that can be stored away: it doubles as a hanging timber feature behind the wall of the barbecue. In keeping with the theme of the garden it is trimmed with a stainless steel band.

THE FANTASTIC THING ABOUT RUNNING WATER
OVER PERFORATIONS OR FINE GROOVES IS THAT
IT CREATES FRICTION, SO WHEN IT'S LIT AT NIGHT
THE STREAM APPEARS TO MOVE IN SLOW MOTION.

COURTYARD OASIS

The commission came from a woman with a busy career living in a small inner-city terrace. The house had recently undergone an interior renovation and the client wanted to continue this new look in the courtyard garden that was no bigger than an average bedroom. Since the living area was extremely small it seemed the best way to go was to add another fully functional room to the house – a room without a roof.

The surrounding properties already provided a considerable amount of privacy so the job came down to dressing the walls and creating a tranquil retreat while making the space feel as large as possible.

A wide cap (the top course on the brickwork) on the edge of the garden bed doubles as informal seating, and a white pebble border on the paving adds light and texture to the ground plan. Plant choice was simple: black bamboo in the garden beds that rim the southern and eastern boundaries, with the lower foliage pulled back to expose the black trunks and expand the space.

The interior hallway has a direct view out into the courtyard presenting a great opportunity to create a focal point that is visible as soon as you enter the house. The vertical stone niche – narrow and discrete to take full advantage of that view from inside – was inspired by the black bamboo stems. Cut out of the engaged pier (a structural row of bricks set into the existing wall for added strength), the niche is laid with polished black stone and finished with a perforated stainless steel strip. A column of water runs down the face of the perforation filling the pond at the base. The fantastic thing about running water over perforations or fine grooves is that it creates friction, so when it's lit at night the stream appears to move in slow motion. It's mesmerising.

TRICKS FOR EXPANDING SMALLER SPACES

There are a few basic tricks for making the most of challenging smaller spaces:

Use a light-coloured border on the perimeter of the paving. This may come in the form of a border tile, a row of pebbles or gravel, or pale foliage on a border planting. The same effect can be achieved by illuminating the perimeter with either tube or spot lighting.

Choose vertical narrow foliage that allows plenty of light to filter through. Bamboos, grasses and strappy, erect foliage such as flax, dietes or iris are ideal.

When positioned correctly, mirrors can bring light into the garden and reflect key points, making the space look double in size.

Always try to use the largest possible format for pavers and tiles to reduce grout lines and simplify the ground plane. If tiling is your choice and mould or tannin from dead leaf-matter is not a problem, a pale grout will also make quite a difference.

Restrict the number of plant varieties. A simple, flowing landscape in a single form helps promote the illusion of space.

Bench seating is the best way to deal with tight areas. It's flexible and tends to hug the perimeter of the paving so it doesn't intrude on the main 'stage' while it softens the gradient in the retaining walls.

Ensure paving or tiles are a lighter shade, but not so bright that they are reflective. This applies to the colour of fences and walls, too.

This range of furniture was designed for the entrance and pool areas of a group of new apartments. The narrow, oiled jarrah slats are ideal for curves: the more slender the format, the softer the curve. The steel frames have a powder-coated black finish to dampen the metallic gleam and all the fixings are stainless steel.

By the pool, an extended bench accommodates up to four people with a wide dip in the middle to give it a comfortable, inviting look. The benches beside the entrance-way paths are similar in form (without the dip) but the lumbar supports curve back on themselves in a modern interpretation of a traditional cylindrical cushion.

BALCONY LANDSCAPE

No matter how small the space, a carefully
planned balcony garden can add a fresh
new dimension to urban living. This inner-city
apartment boasting a fresh, minimal style had
a north-facing balcony that needed a quick
dress-up for a limited budget.

A row of dwarf papyrus nestling in several
custom-built copper planters runs along the
northern perimeter. This plant is perfect for a
balcony situation like this: its upright foliage keeps
it space-efficient and its many finely spiked heads
catch the light throughout the day. Larger and
more upright copper planters bursting with shade-
loving *Ficus lyrata* fill the balcony corners. At the
front edge sit two planters filled with *Yucca
elephantipes*, a stunning architectural plant that
looks great against a neutral background.

A timber trellis is fixed on the eastern wall to
accommodate a Madagascar jasmine that twines
its way across the room. The timber is finished
with copper-style paint, washed back with acid to
give the illusion of a solid piece of warm metal. On
the other side sits the owner's precious antique
Indian chest. With its clean lines and exquisitely
carved surface it really steals the show.

HARBOUR REFLECTIONS

The architect on this split-level apartment had done an impeccable job with the interiors and the property had everything going for it except for access. Lodged at the foot of a steep slope, the only way in was a flight of 400 stairs or a rickety old inclinator. I was acutely conscious of keeping to the budget because whatever I dreamed up would instantly double in price when the contractors saw how difficult it was to get onto the site.

A highlight of the interior design is black granite tiles on the floors so we extended them out into the courtyard to create a sense of continuity between inside and out. The mirror-like properties of this material add a whole new dimension – a 'borrowed landscape' as we call it – reflecting a dreamy image of foliage and sky.

As a windbreak and a safety barrier to the steep drop below, a hedge of *Murraya paniculata* runs along the eastern border. Lily turf (*Liriope muscari*) hides the stems of the *Murraya* forming a soft terrace and, in front of the liriope, along the entire width of the courtyard, is a recessed stainless steel trough. Water enters at the shallow end of the run and trickles through a river of black polished stones to the deep end where there is a recirculating pump in the reservoir.

On the northern side of the garden a small, flat copper bowl constantly overflows, seeping through black stone to a reservoir fringed with black bromeliads and a fine moss-like ground cover called baby's tears. The simple stainless steel and jarrah slat-form bench is positioned for maximum enjoyment of the harbour view and shielded from wind and prying eyes with a grove of towering black bamboo.

ECO THEATRE

Every year I design for garden shows in Australia and overseas. They are a great opportunity to go a bit wild as there are very few restrictions and often a generous budget. In this case, I was able to use the installation as a platform for something I feel very strongly about: bringing recycling and sustainability into the residential garden.

Most of the materials were chosen for their ability to engage with natural processes so that rusting, fading, wearing and decay could add their unique charms to the character of metal, stone and timber.

The main feature of the garden is a 3-metre-high, curved amphitheatre constructed from recyclable steel. Its sinuous, organic curves, with water features at either end, contrast with the rigidity of the rusted steel. The terrace swells to form a seat with a backrest in renewable plantation forest timber. A series of curved steel terraces in the amphitheatre wall form a grid which seems to melt away as the water run increases, gushing between frosted glass into the steel squares below.

Timber columns salvaged from an Auckland recycling yard mark the boundary of the garden in a feature I called the 'Dead Forest'. Like silent sentries, they represent former forests that have been decimated by logging and clearing. Words relating to environmental impact are carved into the wood and, between the timber columns, horizontal chutes of Perspex are filled with black sand, a mining by-product.

Outside the amphitheatre, splayed stepping pads of recycled hardwood form a path through the grey-green pebbles of Marototo endosite. Random cuts of schist (a common New Zealand stone) form the pedestrian path through the interior. The delicate nature of this stone leaves it vulnerable to wear and serves as a reminder to tread the earth lightly.

The internal terraces of the amphitheatre are planted with rows of New Zealand's *Fuchsia procumbens* and *Pratia angulata*. Two thousand seeded *Cosmos bipinnatus* in full flower provide drifts of coloured foliage to soften the towering geometric columns.

AN AMPHITHEATRE EXPERIENCE REFLECTING ON PAST MISUSE OF OUR NATURAL RESOURCES

2
WATER

Water

No prizes for guessing, I love a water feature!

Like so many Australian kids, I was a water baby, drawn like a magnet to creeks and rivers, completely at home in the ocean, and my folks always had a hard time getting me out of the bath. I was fascinated by the things water could do, spending hours building wonky little dams at the local creek and elaborate sandcastles with vast moat systems at the beach. One of the biggest perks of my job is I get to indulge this childhood obsession almost every day.

No matter how stylised, minimal or eccentric a garden, everyone desires a basic element of nature to be represented in our outdoor spaces. A water feature – whether it's a fountain or a pond or a steady trickle down a wall – is the simplest way to provide this. In days gone by, landscape designers like Capability Brown constructed ornate fountains and grand lakes and created ingeniously intricate water systems using gravity and water pressure to power them. Technology has vastly improved and the increasing demand for new ways to bring water into our gardens has meant we now have many choices. Dozens of off-the-shelf fountains are available these days, but I have always preferred to start from scratch.

I'm constantly experimenting with new shapes and textures for water to run through, over and around, and I've used stone, glass, copper, stainless steel, wood and even fabric in water features. There's a practical element to consider as well: the splash of free-falling water can be intrusive to the neighbours when inner-city dwellings are in close proximity. It's important to keep them happy too.

When I think of great water gardens, I think of Indonesia. It's one of my favourite places in the world and one of the strongest influences on my work. A dream of mine is to one day build a house there, with a spectacular garden, of course. During the rainy season there's an abundance of the wet stuff so Indonesians are experts at incorporating water into the garden and planting gardens in water. The unusual combinations and clever arrangement of plants is subtle but effective, and the drip and trickle of myriad waterways give a sense of peace.

Water transforms a garden, and there's a myriad ways of using it: it might be a pool large enough for lap-swimming, a creative solution for a damp area, bringing the beach home with echoes of sand and dunes, or shaping your garden around a harbour view. And no space is too small or too inaccessible to contain a water feature. It takes some careful planning (nobody wants a stagnant pond that breeds mosquitoes), but with the right temperatures, choice of plants and degree of oxygenation, water gardens can exist in perfect harmony with nature and look fresh and beautiful all the time.

NOTHING CAN QUITE COMPETE WITH THE SOOTHING SOUND OF RUNNING WATER TO PROMOTE A FEELING OF REPOSE.

STONEMASON

Talk about a rock and a hard place! This garden was in a marvellous location overlooking a meandering network of waterways, and the clients' request was simple: they wanted a swimming pool. Trouble was, the yard was largely taken up with enormous slabs of sandstone that ascended steeply from the back door and provided very little privacy. Access from the road was also difficult for contractors and would weigh heavily on the available budget. I resolved to turn the difficulties around, and draw upon the good points for inspiration.

Numerous recces were made to the property and I recorded as many levels as possible to establish the best place for the pool to be dug so the builders wouldn't be jack-hammering until the next millennium. The level change in the property was so dramatic it eliminated the need for a pool fence across the leading edge of the swimming pool, but because there were small children in the house, a glass gate was installed at the side.

The original sandstone shelves, framed with rendered retaining walls, are a dramatic backdrop to the pool and plants. Sandstone is shot through with distinctive purple hues due to its mineral content, and these flashes of colour are picked out in the dreamy aubergine shade of the walls. All the niches in the rock are filled with a range of succulents such as agave and echeveria. An upper landing on the top of the sandstone, with pebbles underfoot and some hardy foliage, is a great spot to take in the view.

A row of prickly cycads along the front wall of the pool deters young children from the edge. Rimming the waterline are frosted-glass mosaic tiles and again the combination of colours echoes the sandstone highlights.

The lawn in front of the pool is ideal as a play area for the children. A large yucca and a euphorbia retained from the original garden are the focus of the main garden bed with other foliage shaped around them.

Sometimes the biggest problem in a garden can turn out to be the greatest asset. It's all about focusing on a vision at the beginning of the job and not deviating from the path.

A LARGE YUCCA IN FULL
FLOWER IS A DRAMATIC FOCUS
IN THE MAIN GARDEN BED.

WATER WORDS

Designed by a talented young architect, this is the dream home of a professional couple approaching retirement. They have fairly traditional tastes, but are incredibly sharp and open to new ideas so for me it was a question of successfully blending the conventional with the contemporary.

Recently established, the front garden is reasonably large, so a dense hedge of viburnum across the west-facing wall adds privacy. The front gate bisects this wall and the entrance path meanders past a central pond planted with papyrus and arum lilies with an elevated side that creates a spill-over feature. The southern side of the pond backs onto a grove of gardenia, and a crab apple directly opposite gives shade to a small rendered bench and a grove of standard robinias that form a dense aerial hedge.

The rear courtyard is dominated by a 6-metre water-run, framed with a concrete architrave that extends from the top of the second storey. To embellish the expanse of wall, Madagascar jasmine chases stainless steel cables, drawing attention to elegant stainless steel gutters. Viewing benches oversee the tennis court.

On the south side of the house the bathroom looked out on a dark, dreary patch of earth. It was the perfect spot for some unique artworks the couple had been saving: a pair of Aboriginal totem poles brought back from the far north of Arnhem Land. A sea of pale quartz runs up to the poles, which are set in a base of darker stones, and some black bromeliads introduce a living element.

At the northern entrance, a unique water feature fits snuggly into the brickwork. An English stonemason was commissioned to carve a beautiful Latin inscription into the smooth face of a slate tablet, translated as: Fountain more glistening than crystal. Water falls in silky sheets across the fine lettering making the words gleam and flicker with life.

Water falls in silky sheets across the fine lettering making the words gleam and flicker with life.

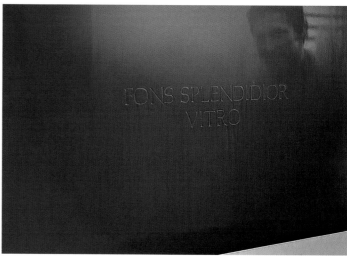

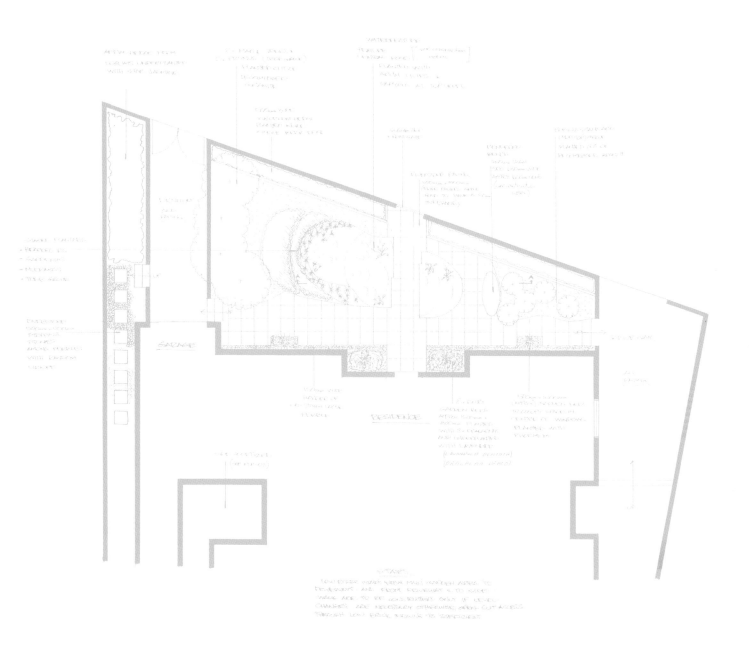

*The pond has an elevated side,
creating a curtain of water that
spills onto the lilypads below.*

The view from the bathroom now takes in these beautiful poles from Arnhem Land.

DESIGN KEY

The wall fountain is constructed out of 20-30 mm 'anvil' granite pebbles fixed to the brick wall with cement, and surrounded by moulded concrete architraves. These architraves are painted with limewash that was mixed to complement the 'tortoise' shade of the house.

12-volt, 50-watt pillar lights.

White quartz and chocolate pebbles ranging from 20-30 mm to 100-150 mm.

The pond is rendered then sealed with Silasec.

500 mm x 500 mm x 45 mm concrete pavers in 'bluestone' colour.

Plants

1 Madagascar Jasmine *Stephanotis floribunda*
2 Dwarf Bull Bay Magnolia *Magnolia grandiflora* 'Little Gem'
3 Gardenia *Gardenia augusta*
4 Water Lily *Nymphaea* sp.
5 Bougainvillea *Bougainvillea* sp.

NOT PICTURED HERE
One Day Iris *Dietes vegeta*
Dragon Tree *Dracaena draco*
French Lavender *Lavandula dentata*
Arum Lily *Zantedeschia aethiopica*
Green Mop Top Robinia *Robinia pseudoacacia* 'Frisia'
Port Wine Magnolia *Michelia figo* 'Bubbles'
Ornamental Grape *Vitis vinifera*
Voodoo Bromeliad *Neoregelia* 'Voodoo'
Papyrus *Cyperus papyrus*

GO WITH THE FLOW

What to do with a gloomy 3.5-metre sandstone wall facing two storeys of glass at the rear of an otherwise beautiful home? The owners were tired of staring at this grim, damp surface covered in patches of unsightly moss. Leaching and constantly wet, it made sense to go with what nature had already provided and turn it into a water wall.

A newly rendered surface was moulded into the contours of the exposed bedrock. Sandstone blocks broken off the original wall are fixed to the new surface, and reflect the mixture of traditional and contemporary in the house's interior.

White stone shelves are pinned at random points across the wall with water trickling over them from three stainless steel emitters placed at even intervals.

A 9-metre-long marine grade aluminium trough was custom-built to span the base. It made a spectacular entrance: delivered on the back of a full-sized semi-trailer. Over the top of the trough sits a steel grate, and this is covered with pebbles to form a natural-looking riverbed. A float switch, which automatically tops up the water level, ensures that the pond stays full, and small halogen lights pick up the water streaming over the rocks.

A wide river of white pebbles, planted out with a selection of bromeliads, *Tnanthe* 'greystar', *Acorus gramineus* 'Ogon' and orchids, hugs the base of the wall, and the pattern of the pale green pavers is broken up with a random arrangement of mosaic lime and quartz pebbles.

This 'problem' wall was not so much rebuilt as restructured, transforming a dank and oppressive outlook into a bright, light feature, projecting colour, movement and a gentle blend of old and new.

BUSHLAND EXOTICA

One of the owners of this lovely property had spent a lot of time in the travel industry before she switched to interior designing. The result of this fusion of careers is an eclectic mix of Indian, Moroccan and Greek influences in her home. 'I designed the house so that the interior and the garden meld into one,' she said. 'It's hard to tell where the house finishes and the garden begins.' I couldn't agree more. My task was to create a water feature to complement the existing pool.

The owner had recently installed bench seating and a barbecue area to make the space more useful, surrounding the pool with a frameless glass fence. My innovation was the feature wall that dominates the southern side of the pool. I selected a series of hardy quartz pebbles ranging from 20–30 mm to 75–100 mm. The final mosaic groups the pebbles into a series of mounds that bring to mind the small volcanic geysers found at hot springs. Water streams from a concealed pipe at the top of the wall, meanders through the glistening mounds and melts into the pool.

The large *Phoenix canariensis* already located on the other side of the garden balances the water feature with its thick robust trunk and generous canopy. At the far end of the pool, the land erupts into dense natural bush, providing a magical backdrop for this oasis by the sea.

The frameless glass fence around the pool acts as
a windbreak and, most importantly, a safety barrier.

SEASIDE RETREAT

Close to the beach, this apartment had it all: great views, perfect location and a complete interior makeover, but the garden was virtually non-existent. I began with my customary routine: going through all the rooms making notes on the position of windows and access points. Then I went around and sat in all the chairs, checked out the kitchen and even lay on the bed to ascertain all the viewpoints in the place. Making the garden work for these perspectives is kind of like window dressing, the difference being it's permanent and the view is forever changing with the seasons.

The garden bed has as its centrepiece a glossy dense shrub called port wine magnolia *(Michelia figo)* which exudes the most delectable scent in the evenings. Along the front of the bed, a slim stainless steel trough contains a stream of running water fringed with *Liriope muscari*. Four evenly spaced stacks of slate and glass sit in the trough, each with a small fountain bubbling merrily at the summit.

The L-shaped kitchen and seating area with convenient benchtops and a built-in barbecue are designed for outdoor entertaining. To conjure up the beach nearby, all the timber is white-washed and sealed to look like weathered driftwood.

Lines of timber trellis fixed at random points along the north wall accommodate an espaliered camellia with fresh ivory blooms. Ponytail palms sprout from built-in planters that interrupt the benches and clumps of Cordyline (*Cordyline fruticosa* 'Rubra') introduce everlasting sprays of crimson.

The perfect place to relax and unwind after a hard day at the beach.

THE SECRET OF GREAT GARDEN DESIGN IS NOT SO MUCH IN THE ELEMENTS YOU USE, IT'S IN HOW YOU PUT THEM TOGETHER.

LIGHT TOWERS

Set into a hillside in a leafy suburb, this grand Tuscan-style house overlooked a lush semi-tropical garden that fell away to a huge pool area below. There was a lot of potential in this rather neglected space: it was already screened well for privacy, the pool was unusually large and there was a disused cabana to one side crying out for a makeover.

The paving was discoloured and choked with leaf matter and parts of it were cracked and broken. It needed to be replaced with a stain-resistant surface that would be more temperate for bare feet and able to drain well. Hardwood timber decking fulfilled the requirements and the client liked it so much that we continued it up the wall at one end, creating a 'wave' of wood. To break up the expanse of timber, steel rills were cut through the decking at five points to carry the water from the towers into the pool.

Three tower light features, each over 3.5 metres in height, are constructed from steel, timber and glass along the east side of the pool with clouds of Chilean jasmine (*Mandevilla* sp.) spilling from the top. Strong upward lights glow through the glass panels and a mirror inside the tower reflects and evens out the light source. The exteriors are dressed with timber battens at graduating intervals across the panes of glass, sectioning the radiant light to create a striped effect. A reservoir expels a stream of water that runs down the glass into a trough and eventually into the pool. Facing the light towers is a timber day-bed flanked with benches and custom-built copper planters holding large ensephilatas.

Three split-level pontoons were built at the north end of the pool, one of which was cantilevered over the edge of the water to make a diving board. These mini-platforms are a kind of magnet, enticing the pool-user to sunbathe or use them as diving-off points. Kentia palms (*Howea forsteriana*) and cycads grow through holes cut in the decking to provide green interludes.

A timber staircase descends from the top level directly into the pool. As it hits the water the stair supports become stainless steel and the timber changes to tallow wood. These two materials work better than any others in wet conditions.

DON'T FORGET THE BORROWED
LANDSCAPE – THE TREES AND
SHRUBS THAT YOU CAN SEE
OVER THE FENCE IN YOUR
NEIGHBOUR'S GARDEN. THEY
EXPAND THE VISUAL IMPACT OF
YOUR GARDEN AND ADD SHADE
AND SHADOWS.

EDGE OF THE WORLD

This is the kind of job designers dream about. A breathtaking location on the tip of a Sydney Harbour bay overlooking the sparkling water and majestic Sydney Harbour Bridge. The house itself is a superbly realised architectural structure with panoramic views from every level. Despite the aesthetic backdrop it was going to be a challenge for me in terms of space. The house sprawls across most of the land and my brief included an in-ground pool, a cabana and a patio.

First priority was the pool. It was extended from the house to the boundary of the property and surrounded with lustrous white limestone. The sea-side is finished with a 'wet-edge' so the water gently laps over into a catchtank below. With the harbour just beyond the horizon, the pool appears to melt seamlessly over the lip into the bay – a stunning visual effect. On the north-east side, the specially commissioned sculpture of a large steel globe catches the sun and makes a fantastic conversation piece.

Something out of the ordinary was needed for the garden beds and there was quite a stir in the neighbourhood when trucks and crane arrived with the latest horticultural additions. Two enormous 12-year-old frangipani trees were hoisted over the sandstone walls into pre-prepared holes between the dwelling and the pool where their creamy blossoms now perfume the air during the warmer months. On the north-west side of the house, a 40-year-old *Dracaena draco* almost nine metres high is a perfect visual contrast to the stark white wall behind it made up of hundreds of powder-coated aluminium tiles. The three mature 'bring-ins' required excellent drainage and were braced for more than a year so that the root system was mature enough to render them structurally sound. Beneath the *Dracaena draco* a herb garden now thrives and the other featured beds (entrance and rear) were filled with plants suitable for the coastal location: bromeliads, ornamental grasses and palms, box hedge, camellia, bird of paradise and gardenia.

Years on, this glorious home continues to draw gasps of appreciation from passing traffic – land and sea – and I feel very fortunate that I was able to play a part in enhancing its natural beauty.

DUNE GARDEN

Built entirely on sand, this coastal design garden was a special display at the Melbourne International Flower and Garden Show and drew a great deal of interest and discussion.

Sand feels great underfoot, and as long as there is no problem with erosion and weeds are kept under control, there is no reason why it can't be used as a garden landscape surface.

As a kid I spent many summers down at the beach and I have vivid memories of hopping along timber sleepers chained together to escape the baking hot sand. The splayed finger-like steppers you see here are a direct descendant of those sleepers, forming an unusual pathway and guarding against erosion.

The entranceway is a striking galvanised frame suspended on recycled telegraph poles that have been aged by the elements. Tea tree sticks spanning the frame act as a light filter with a series of pontoons underneath. The pontoons are built from large solid timber sleepers and are treated so they are not susceptible to dry rot and vermin.

White stones hang like strings of shells at the entrance, continuing the beach theme. This feature was quite an episode to organise. First I had to find somebody willing to drill holes in stones, and I finally managed to persuade a granite supplier to take it on. I dropped them off at the guy's workshop and he phoned me – four broken diamond-tipped drill bits (imported especially from Germany) and 384 pebbles later – saying, 'My hands are bleeding. Come and get your pebbles. I've had enough!' The job was fantastic, but I did feel a little guilty.

To give privacy to the garden but still allow the view, the fence is a series of vertical timber slats run on an angle with the spacings progressively widening as the ocean view unfolds. For background colour, a stunning weathered-look tangerine orange (reminds me of a tropical ocean sunset) was painted on the rear walls.

A curved timber day-bed tapers off to provide a bench for up to four people. It's a tight curve and, to manage the length, timber slats are laid on edge. The bench keeps the same form but drops to 100 mm above ground level where it becomes the base grill for an outdoor shower with a generous showerhead.

Behind the day-bed is a tea tree – a salt-tolerant and famously hardy native which is ideal for coastal conditions. White granite pebbles and boulders are scattered at random over the sand and clumps of gazania provide splashes of bold colour.

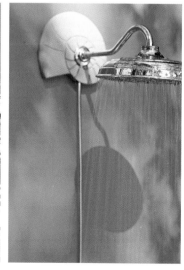

DESIGN KEY

The showerhead connects to the wall with a custom-made shell design cut to shape out of a 20 mm fibre cement sheeting.

External limewash in burnt orange, 'astrid's madras'

The planters are mild steel containers with a sealed interior. They are open to the earth at the base to enable the roots to penetrate the ground.

The frame of the shade structure is constructed from galvanised steel and powder-coated, cantilevered recycled telegraph poles that are 300 mm in diameter. A stainless-steel cable runs between 25-40 mm poles made from rustic tea tree.

The pontoons are constructed from 200 mm x 70 mm treated pine. These sleepers are okay for in-ground use with a treatment to a level of H5 to stop insects and rotting.

The fences are built from 90 mm x 19 mm treated pine in vertical slat form with spacings that begin at 25 mm and spread to 125 mm, all slats set at 45˚.

This bench is a recycled pier, 500 mm x 400 mm. Check out your local recycled timber yard or demolition yard for bits and pieces like these that can be used in interesting ways.

Plants

1 Treasure Flower *Gazania* sp.
2 Swamp Foxtail Grass *Pennisetum alopecuroides*
3 Bird of Paradise *Strelitzia reginae*
4 Dragon Tree *Dracaena draco*

NOT PICTURED HERE

Yucca *Yucca elephantipes*

Lemon Scented Tea Tree *Leptospermum petersonii*

1

4

2

3

3
PEOPLE

People

'We need a place outside where we can have dinner with our friends.' 'I love to veg out on the couch reading the paper but there's nowhere to do that in my garden.' 'We've got a barbecue in the backyard but Jim's always way down there cooking and everyone else is congregating around the table.'

When the business first started I was bombarded by comments like these. I found myself jotting down all the mod-cons, time-savers and comfortable luxuries that we have in our homes like heaters, lounges, showers, bathtubs, chopping surfaces and game boards. The search was on for new ways to re-create these facilities outside and I guess I've been experimenting ever since.

These days in place of the lounge suite there are rendered benches with soft cushions and long timber seats with comfortable lumbar supports. Kitchen essentials are reproduced and materials altered to withstand the elements. You'll find sinks in granite benchtops, stainless steel hotplates and splashbacks, under-bench cupboards for storage and subtle overhead lighting.

But garden entertaining is not just about outdoor loungerooms and kitchens, it's also about recreation. Pools, spas, chessboards, volleyball, tennis and even basketball courts are all part of the entertaining experience. The trick is to make everything look as if it belongs in the garden. If an outdoor kitchen or lounge space is installed in the right way with a garden that complements it, you suddenly have an asset that is both attractive and valuable.

Pool companies and builders are increasingly aware of the importance of good garden design and how the relationship between plants and pool can be central to its success. Outdoor showers are becoming a standard feature in my designs for houses that are located close to the beach or have their own pool area. The client may be sceptical at first, but they invariably come back to me saying, 'I can't believe how often it gets used!' And finally, let's not forget the long-term advantage of improving your property's exterior living area. One of the first things most home buyers will do at an inspection is head to the recreational spaces so they can picture themselves relaxing in their potential home, so it's worth the investment.

An important part of my design strategy is to play with the levels of a courtyard or al fresco dining area because it instantly creates a feeling of intimacy. Have you ever wondered why it feels so good to walk into a sunken room? The walls suddenly seem higher, as if they are almost cradling you, and the submerged space encourages us to sit closer together. I believe that same cosy feeling can be achieved outdoors. It can be as simple as raising the garden beds or staging the levels of planting from small at the front to tall at the back, creating an amphitheatre effect.

Benches, spas, lounges, pools, table settings and a host of other wonderful features act as magnets drawing us into the garden. As long as we all yearn to spend more time in the great outdoors we will continue inventing new ideas and reasons to enjoy the gifts of our beautiful climate.

SPA TO SEA

My lifestyle is fairly similar to that of the owners of this house, and the garden was a joy to design from beginning to end. I have to admit to experiencing pangs of garden envy whenever I see the place now.

Location was a major factor, as the property sits on one of the most picturesque ocean view sites I have ever seen. Although the land area is quite large, the house takes up most of the site, so my goal was to make the garden feel long, generous and open, create a sense of privacy (especially in the entertaining area), and make sure the garden didn't overpower the spectacular view. The ocean is so close it feels like a part of the property and I wanted to extend the sight, smell and sound of water throughout the garden. In front of the house, the swimming pool is the farthest possible point from the ocean so my plan was to link the two elements together with water tumbling down through the garden towards the sea.

At the highest point of the land, with an uninterrupted view of the horizon, we built a large customised spa, flanked by deck and garden. A contoured sun lounge for four is built from the same timber as the deck. The spa and pool are surrounded with sun-loving plants, like bird of paradise, jasmine, golden barrel cacti, yuccas and euphorbia. Black sand mulch accentuates the colour of the foliage and minimises plant maintenance.

One of the most successful aspects of this garden is the illusion that the water flowing through the garden is fed by the spa. The liquid journey begins at the spa, which steadily overflows into a pond at the base and in turn spills over a copper lip and onto the face of a glistening sheet of structural glass. Different-sized copper strips were placed at random intervals on its surface to create water disturbance. The glass is front- and back-lit to make the most of the action of the drop and when the water lands in the catch pond it splits into two different directions.

On stage left, the water flows into a copper river channel that gently laps around five palm trees that look as if they've been planted in their own islands. Their root balls extend beneath the water channel, otherwise they would become drenched and quickly rot.

On stage right, the water tumbles over a series of five weirs that are back-lit and softened by cream leadlight panels. In each of the five ponds

sits a copper bowl, every one of them spun out of a single piece of copper (it's a dying art but luckily my old friend Ralph is a genius at such techniques). The bowls are positioned on the surface of the water as if they are floating, and the echeveria planted inside draws moisture through the base. With water peeling off the steps in a single continuous sheet, the backdrop for these bowls is enchanting.

The two water trails mingle once again in a huge concrete balance tank under the lawn.

Bench-seating for up to 40 people lines one side of the garden, with stone tablets placed at intervals to break up the space. The tablets are beautiful light features and form the base for fine pieces of sculpture that are up-lit by small halogen lights recessed in the stone. Timber for the benches is profiled in a small format to elongate the form and give it a sleek, contemporary look similar to the furniture in the house. Small curved timber lumbar supports serve as comfortable back rests.

Stainless steel cables run along the tops of the sandstone walls guiding jasmine along the boundary to create more privacy. Specially constructed copper planters house beds of annuals, and a row of yuccas is planted in a large copper retaining wall at the end of the pool.

On the upstairs balcony, another row of yuccas in a copper trough shields the bedroom for more privacy. In the corner is a low, self-contained water feature: a copper trough encloses a sandstone plinth that is fitted with cantilevered, frosted resin tablets. These hold turned wooden spheres lined with copper that spill steady liquid trails. The feature looks fantastic lit up at night.

The garden is a triumph, both aesthetically and in practice. The owners love to show it off to their friends and in the warmer months they almost live outside. To me that's the highest praise of all.

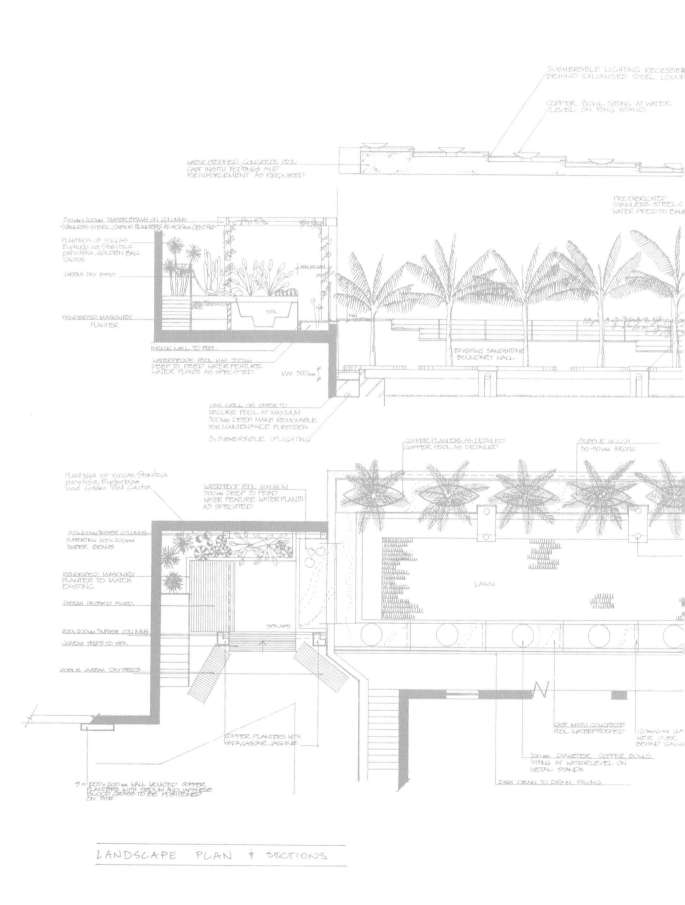

SUBMERSIBLE LIGHTING RECESSED
BEHIND GALVANISED STEEL LOUVRE

COPPER BOWL SITTING AT WATER
LEVEL ON RING STAND

WATER PROOFED CONCRETE POOL
CAST INSITU. FOOTINGS AND
REINFORCEMENT AS REQUIRED

PRE-FABRICATED
STAINLESS STEEL
WATER PIPED TO BAI

200mm x 200mm TIMBER BEAMS ON COLUMNS
STAINLESS STEEL CABLE PLANTERS AT 400mm CENTRES

PLANTINGS OF YUCCAS
Euphodo, os, Strelitzia
parvifolia, GOLDEN BALL
CACTUS

JARRAH DAY BED

RENDERED MASONRY
PLANTER

BRICK WALL TO POOL.

WATERPROOF POOL MAX. 300mm
DEEP TO FEED WATER FEATURE
WATER PLANTS AS SPECIFIED

MAX 300mm

USE GRILL OR OTHER TO
SECURE POOL AT MAXIMUM
300mm DEEP MAKE REMOVABLE
FOR MAINTENANCE PURPOSES

3x SUBMERSIBLE UPLIGHTING

EXISTING SANDSTONE
BOUNDARY WALL

COPPER PLANTERS AS DETAILED
COPPER POOL AS DETAILED

PEBBLE MULCH
30-50 MM AROMIC

PLANTINGS OF YUCCAS, Strelitzia
parvifolia, Euphorbias
and Golden Ball Cactus.

WATERPROOF POOL MAXIMUM
200mm DEEP TO FEED
WATER FEATURE WATER PLANTS
AS SPECIFIED

200x200mm TIMBER COLUMNS
SUPPORTING 200x200mm
TIMBER BEAMS

RENDERED MASONRY
PLANTER TO MATCH
EXISTING

JARRAH DAYBED FIXED.

200x200mm TIMBER COLUMNS

JARRAH STEPS TO SPA

MOBILE JARRAH DAYBEDS

LAWN

SPA STEPS

CAST INSITU CONCRETE
POOL WATERPROOFED

120mm GA
WEIR OVER
BEHIND GALVA

COPPER PLANTERS WITH
MADAGASCAR JASMINE

300mm DIAMETER COPPER BOWLS
SITTING AT WATERLEVEL ON
METAL STANDS

5 x 1000 x 200 mm WALL MOUNTED COPPER
PLANTERS WITH SEDUM AND JAPANESE
BLOOD GRASS TO BE POSITIONED
ON SITE.

DISH DRAIN TO DRAIN PAVING

LANDSCAPE PLAN & SECTIONS

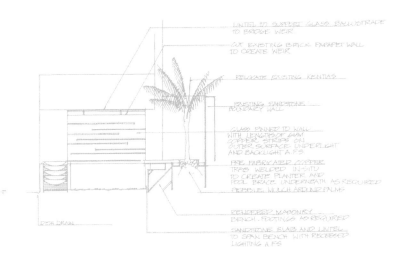

LINTEL TO SUPPORT GLASS BALUSTRADE TO BRIDGE WEIR

CUT EXISTING BRICK PARAPET WALL TO CREATE WEIR

RELOCATE EXISTING KENTIAS

EXISTING SANDSTONE BOUNDARY WALL

GLASS FIXED TO WALL WITH LENGTHS OF 6MM COPPER STRIPS ON OUTER SURFACE UNDERLIGHT AND BACKLIGHT A FS

PRE FABRICATED COPPER TRAYS WELDED IN SITU TO CREATE PLANTER AND POOL BRACE UNDERNEATH AS REQUIRED

PEBBLE MULCH AROUND PALMS

RENDERED MASONRY BENCH FOOTINGS AS REQUIRED

SANDSTONE SLAB AND LINTEL TO SPAN BENCH WITH RECESSED LIGHTING A FS

DISH DRAIN

RELOCATE EXISTING PALMS

STAINLESS STEEL CABLE TRELLIS WITH MADAGASCAR JASMINE

SANDSTONE SLABS WITH RECESSED LIGHTING AFS

COPPER PLANTERS AS DETAILED

RENDERED MASONRY SEAT FOOTINGS AS REQUIRED

LAWN

STAINLESS STEEL CABLE TRELLIS MADAGASCAR JASMINE

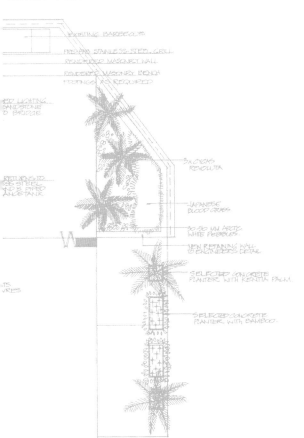

EXISTING BARBECUE

RECESSED STAINLESS STEEL GRILL

RENDERED MASONRY WALL

RENDERED MASONRY BENCH FOOTINGS AS REQUIRED

UNDER LIGHTING SANDSTONE TO BRIDGE

3X CYCAS REVOLUTA

JAPANESE BLOOD GRASS

30-50 MM ARCTIC WHITE PEBBLES

1M RETAINING WALL TO ENGINEERS DETAIL

SELECTED CONCRETE PLANTER WITH KENTIA PALM

SELECTED CONCRETE PLANTER WITH BAMBOO

RETURNS TO 316 STEEL AND IS PIPED ANTE TANK

DESIGN KEY

The plinths are carved from Sydney sandstone by artist and stonemason Michael Purdy.

The benches are built from 45 mm x 19 mm hardwood (Kwila) slats.

1.6 m copper sheeting with black sand as mulch

Limewash Boncote paint, 'venetian green'

The pergola is constructed from piers of recycled ironbark fixed with stainless steel stirrups. The cables are fixed with stainless steel turnbuckles and run between the beams at 400 mm intervals.

50-75 mm 'Anvil' granite pebbles

These copper bowls are spun from 1.6 mm copper sheets into 600 mm diameter x 160 mm depth. They feature a safety edge and are filled with black sand as mulch.

Fluorescent 240-volt globe lights in the risers of the steps are filtered with beige opaque glass for a subtle glow

Plants

1 Hen and Chickens Cactus *Echeveria*
2 Madagascar Jasmine *Stephanotis floribunda*
3 Yucca *Yucca elephantipes*
4 African Milk Tree, Green Dragon *Euphorbia trigona*
5 Treasure Flower *Gazania* sp.
6 Golden Barrel Cactus *Echinocactus grusonii*

NOT PICTURED HERE
Small Leafed Strelitzia *Strelitzia reginae* var. *parvifolia*
Mother-in-Law's Tongue *Sansevieria trifasciata*
Sweet Flag *Acorus gramineus* 'Ogon'
Cycad *Cycas revoluta*

PLAYTIME

A healthy crop of weeds and an ancient tumbledown shed was my first impression of this garden. The owners wanted some serious greening up and a place for their grandchildren to play that was fun, safe and didn't cost a lot. When I asked them what kind of activities the children preferred it sounded like they were just as I was at their age – they love water.

A raised patio and some Hebel (aerated concrete) benches allow the family to have meals outdoors or just sit and watch the kids playing. This dining area is surrounded by shallow channels of water flowing along a network of recycled tallow wood beams. Originating from a ramp of stepped green concrete pavers (sealed and waterproofed) the water journeys through the garden to a reflective pond with a 400-mm-deep spillway. The children can interact with every part of this waterway and the owners showed me some great photos of them splashing about enjoying the ramps and mini-waterfalls. A little sandpit was put in for them, too.

On the surface of the pond a white-glazed hibachi bowl is brimming with echeverias, otherwise known as hen and chickens for the way the main plant sprouts tiny round off-shoots. Pale green terraces of *Strelitzia parvifolia* contrast with the deep burgundy foliage of ajugas and the beds are planted out with grass trees (*Xanthorrhoea*), triangle palms (*Neodypsis decarii*) and cordylines. The rest of the garden is mulched with a 'cowra' river pebble making the space light, bright and golden.

Easy to maintain, with lots to see and do, this garden pleases all ages.

LINKING OLD AND NEW

This is a classic Victorian-style house with a modern extension on the rear. Between the house and the workshop at the western end of the property is an L-shaped space with dappled light and sandy soil. The clients wanted a link between the two dwellings: a pleasant, useable space where they could entertain as well as cultivate a large vegetable patch.

At first a series of large stepping-stones seemed like a good way of creating the link, but a deck would also do the job and be a useful platform too. I mixed the two ideas and constructed a series of floating pontoons fixed at slightly different levels.

When faced with structures with a different aesthetic, I find that, as long as the main connecting material goes from door to door (in this case the decking) and the planting is consistent, the link is invariably successful. This same principle is also helpful with odd-sized buildings and strange configurations.

The focal point in the centre of the garden is a large steel planter containing a mature magnolia. The planter was treated so that the steel will only rust to a certain degree and at the same time attain a uniquely weathered finish. An avenue-screen planting of bay trees runs along the southern boundary and the large vegetable patch in front takes full advantage of the sunniest spot in the yard.

Large cordylines in white glazed pots and a majestic robinia tree dominate the north side. Underneath the robinia a long slender aluminium trough spans the garden beds, interrupting the deck and terminating at the courtyard patio. Japanese blood grass frames the water, with dietes and iris spot-planted between the pontoons.

Broken slate is scattered about mulching the whole garden. These scraps gathered from quarries keep the soil moist while allowing it to breathe and of course, it's great to make use of something that otherwise would be discarded as waste.

MATES' RATES

This was an unusual job for me. A good friend asked me to design his garden and, though I don't make a habit of working for mates, I relented because I often spend weekends over there with our gang of mutual friends.

My first decision was to completely break with professional protocol and disregard whatever my mate suggested (I didn't tell him that, of course). He's a persistent guy and proceeded to hover while I played with designs so I told him to go inside. When a job is personal, the pressure's really on!

The 'client' loves to walk around naked when no one's home, so to help out his poor neighbours the walls were raised with more foliage. His house is by the beach so an outdoor shower was also an appropriate addition; that way he could rinse off the sand and validate his nudity at the same time. And he's a big talker, too, so an outdoor kitchen with a sink would definitely come in handy, ensuring he never has to leave the conversation.

Heat was the first major problem. The courtyard catches the full sun all day so it desperately needed a cooling system: water, shade or plant.

'What about the budget for materials?' my mate asked, knowing my impulsive ways.

'Don't worry about it, buddy, you've had a good year, haven't you?' I barked back at him. No way was I going to let him cramp the concept.

And so the fun began ...

The choice of colour and materials was easy. He's Greek so it was no big surprise when he said, 'Lots of white and lots of concrete.' He insisted the text book designers' term for the style he loves is the 'Mediterranean Look' and I told him not to worry – I would give him that and more, for free of course. Okay, maybe for a couple of tubs of his mum's homemade hummus (yes, it's that good).

The courtyard isn't huge but some days it holds up to 20 guests so the garden is bordered with a C-shape run of bench seating to make best use of the available space. A small rill runs behind the entire seating area to give lumbar support. A rill is an ancient form of plumbing, literally a small open gutter that is gouged from the ground alongside a pathway.

To produce a cooling effect, the water feature needed to subtly influence every part of the garden. Originating from three points on the rear wall, it trickles through the entire area, ending at two identical ponds where it is re-circulated. The ponds are connected by an underground pipe to

TODAY WE STILL MARVEL AT THE PLEASURE OF
HAVING TRAILS OF WATER FLOWING AROUND
US – WE MAY BE SITTING IN FULL SUN BUT WE
FEEL COMFORTABLE AND COOL.

ensure they maintain the same depth even if one fills quicker than the other. The rear wall is given an eye-catching contemporary edge with a series of glass tiles. White quartz pebbles are embedded in the water ramps to give the water a texture to travel through. The movement is down-lit by a halogen eyelid spot.

A sun-lounge was custom-built from cedar slats on a stainless steel frame with wheels because my friend is always going on about how he loves to 'follow the sun'. Then he produced a Greek reproduction statue he'd just bought and to my horror demanded I work it into my contemporary design. I found the perfect spot for it down the side of the house where it has a great view of the air conditioner, and to give it even more privacy, I screened it off with some cedar shutters. The same cedar shutters were installed under the black granite benchtops in the outdoor kitchen. These served as cupboards to conceal a vast collection of cleaning products – enough to stock a supermarket. He does have a bit of a fixation about spotless surfaces.

Eight beautiful standard mop-top robinias form a hedge across the rear wall, shielding the western sun and providing extra privacy. This style of hedge is called 'pleached' which means an avenue of standard (usually small-size) trees where the trunks are bare and the canopies join up creating a continuous wall of greenery. It's an old European concept used in many formal gardens to striking effect.

The planting beneath the robinias is Chinese star jasmine, which makes a dense and colourful groundcover, breaking up the concrete so that the garden feels full. This variety is called tri-colour because of the beautiful pink tips on the leaves; it looks good no matter what the season.

A magnificent little gem magnolia found a home on the south-side of the garden and Madagascar jasmine crawls along steel cables at the top of the southern fence to create more privacy. Dwarf and giant papyrus grow in the two catch ponds and two large white crackle-glaze pots containing a couple of superb pink frangipanis adorn either side of the back door. Frangipanis can be planted with great success against brick walls in full sun because the warmth tricks the plants into feeling they are in a more tropical environment.

Pale-green concrete pavers keep the courtyard feeling cool, and I double-sealed them to guard against those tipsy afternoon barbecues when the red wine sloshes over. The moulded concrete table in a plain rectangular shape with tablet legs was selected to keep the palette of materials simple. A dozen woven grass cushions are scattered about to soften the stark white concrete. The warm colour and rippling texture of this organic 'fabric' is perfectly in tune with the surroundings.

It's a couple of years now since I did the job and we've had some great times in this courtyard. My friend often says it has transformed his lifestyle, especially the daily pleasure of taking his morning shower outdoors. And he's never complained about the budget … not yet anyway.

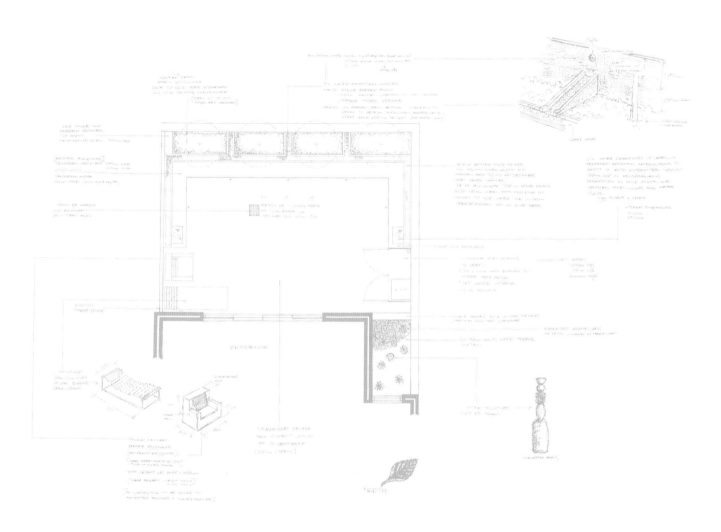

SUN TRAP

With a view as stunning as this one overlooking Sydney Harbour, it's no wonder the clients wanted to do justice to it with a complete makeover of their sprawling balcony. Drenched in sun for most of the day, it was perfect for planting and offered lots of scope for the human occupants, too.

A long rendered bench on the north-west side is designed for entertaining. Above it, the expanse of neutral wall cried out for a feature and I didn't have to look far for inspiration with the sea glinting in the corner of my eye. A stainless steel architrave serves as a sturdy frame, which is filled with an arrangement of white quartz pebbles carefully graded to form an abstract interpretation of a fish spine. At night a small spill of light issues from a tube in the architrave making the fossil-like shape stand out in sharp relief.

On the eastern side is a water feature, made from the same material as the spine sculpture. White quartz pebbles are arranged in an identical architrave but in this instance water trickles down through the pebbles to a glass reservoir where it recirculates. In front of the reservoir stands a small glass trough with special ports to allow drainage for a row of *Liriope muscari*. More glass planters around the balcony hold perennials that are changed over every six months by the owner who is a keen green-thumb.

The reconstituted sandstone bowls at the farthest corners of the balcony were reproduced from moulds taken from two large Balinese water bowls. Brimming with arum lilies and dwarf papyrus they look magical at night with tiny beams of light shining up through the foliage.

For extra seating, stainless steel benches with jarrah timber slat tops and circular bollards as lumbar support are designed to be moved about to suit the occasion.

The balcony room is now a constantly used, flexible space and offers a veritable feast for the senses with the soft music of running water, the delicate perfume of lilies, and of course, the sweeping harbour view.

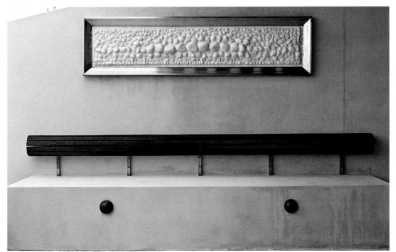

THE BALCONY ROOM IS NOW
A CONSTANTLY USED, FLEXIBLE
SPACE AND OFFERS A VERITABLE
FEAST FOR THE SENSES WITH THE
SOFT MUSIC OF RUNNING WATER,
THE DELICATE PERFUME OF LILIES,
AND OF COURSE, THE SWEEPING
HARBOUR VIEW.

4
PLACES

Places

Years of travelling have had a profound impact on my creative development and I've drawn inspiration from many different cultures. There are, however, specific cultural aesthetics that I return to time and again in my work. I've already talked about my passion for all things Balinese and it comes out again in some of the following gardens. Countries like Mexico and Turkey also have climates that dictate an outdoor lifestyle and you will see how I interpret their particular style in some recent installation gardens.

But if I had to name the culture that has had the strongest impact on my work, it would have to be the Land of the Rising Sun. A typical Japanese garden is a miniature representation of a natural landscape, contrived, planned and executed with precision. Framed by secure dominating walls that shut out the world, it is a private, secluded and often fantastical haven. Stones, carvings, gravels and plant material are all carefully selected and positioned in such a way as to symbolise mountains, forests, rivers and lakes.

When you enter a Japanese garden, it's best to take time and observe the fine white gravels that circle a natural feature, encouraging the eye to savour the intricate beauty of the object. Like an antidote to our too-busy lives, these techniques coax us into admiring something we would generally overlook. Everywhere you look there's a lesson in the relationship between materials, shapes, textures, colours, space and form; all the fundamental elements of design. With drifts of moss, delicate groundcovers, finely manicured shrubs and trees, woven bamboo screens and mosaic pathways, the Japanese have a fantastic way of creating charm and mystery in their gardens. It's a discipline that has been passed down for centuries, and is one of the rare forms of landscaping that has always been respected and rarely compromised.

The principles employed in making a Japanese garden permeate every one of my designs. Sometimes it's the predominant theme, but most of the time it can be found in the quest for simple structure and pure form that is evident in all my work, from a tiny city balcony to an opulent seaside mansion.

GREEN THERAPY

'Relaxing', 'retreat' and 'haven' were words the client used when he described his vision for this garden. The motives behind his desires were both personal and professional: he runs a very successful business in therapeutic services and wanted the outside to reflect the peaceful de-stressing activities that went on inside the house.

Privacy was first priority. A series of partitions erected in a loose arrangement enable parts of the garden to be screened off. These structures take the form of a 2.4-metre high 'doorway' consisting of three robust timber sleepers with sheets of Natureed suspended from the lintels. The panels are an excellent filter – sun streams through the reeds in slender shafts contrasting with the loose dappled light leaking from the surrounding trees. When a soft breeze passes through, it looks as if the garden is dancing.

The entrance way is a sequence of timber sleepers laid side by side to produce a soft-form pathway. Whenever possible, I like to stick to one principal material and use it in as many different ways as possible so here benches, paving, and partitions were all made of timber sleepers.

Water bubbles up through two steel bowls (they look a bit like giant cooking woks!) and overflows, following the graceful curve of the bowl to the pebbles at its base, which conceal the reservoir beneath. The bowls are set perfectly level so the surface of the water remains flat to mirror trees and sky.

The combination of plants is designed to look luscious: with its long stems and fleshy leaves, *Strelitzia nicolai* brings height and volume, ixora adds splashes of tangerine, cycads bring bold shapes, liriope and dietes add texture and tendrils of English ivy and rich purple *Ajuga reptans* make a delicate groundcover.

The owner is so delighted with the results that he holds consultations in the garden whenever possible. Just a few minutes out there and you can actually feel your stress levels go down.

SUN STREAMS THROUGH THE REEDS
IN SLENDER SHAFTS CONTRASTING
WITH THE LOOSE DAPPLED LIGHT
LEAKING FROM THE SURROUNDING
TREES. WHEN A SOFT BREEZE
PASSES THROUGH, IT LOOKS AS
IF THE GARDEN IS DANCING.

TIPS FOR CREATING A SENSE OF INTIMACY

Here are a few tips about how to create privacy,
intimacy and a feeling of security in your garden:

Place vertical timber slats on an angle to act as shutters. These retain light and air flow and give privacy that doesn't obstruct the view.

Take your planting 'up', and use planters in different ways, for example, fix planters on top of a wall for added height and plant them with dense vertical foliage like *Lomandra longifolia*.

Natureed has a world of uses. Supplied as sheets of 4-mm-thick reeds bound together with galvanised wire, it can be placed wherever a light filter is needed. It can disguise unsightly fences and it can serve as a partition, dividing off sections of the garden to create an intimate space.

Think of boundaries not just as fences, but as backdrops for featured plants and installations.

Nothing beats a wall of green for ultimate garden atmosphere, and tall plants will help give your backyard a sense of enclosure. Fast-growing plants like bamboo, murraya, lilly pilly, Leyland cypress and pittosporum are ideal.

Trellised vines, canvas sailcloths and natural fibre screens not only look great, they also block harmful UV-rays and obstruct the view of prying eyes.

LIQUID CURVES

Collaboration was the major factor in designing this suburban garden. When I arrived for the initial consultation, I was met by a busy professional couple, two very cute dogs and a collection of clippings, colour-boards, samples and ideas they'd been gathering for at least two years. As I drove back to the studio that day I knew I had to come up with a concept that would not only fit their very detailed brief but also challenge their rich imaginations.

The furniture in the house is modern, their art is simple and tasteful and everything has its place. I was particularly taken with the picture of wild blue irises in full flower painted on a long screen of silk. Outside, with trusty sketch pad in hand, I wandered the site, doodling with ideas until the image of a sweeping curve of water came to mind. Flanked on one side by a generous rendered bench, it would border two levels of deck and a set of curved terraces as stairs. I quickly ran it by the lady of the house, all the while dreading the words: 'I'll think about it and give you a call.' (This usually means they've got an appointment with another consultant.) To my amazement she was able to understand my rough chicken scratch on paper and loved the concept. The guys at the office quickly drafted it up and the work began.

The deck is built from a small-format ironbark, which will eventually age to a soft dove-grey. So the water can be enjoyed from both levels and viewed from the loungeroom too, a run of pebbles pours down the northern border of the property ending at a pond filled with papyrus and acorus that cuts into the lower deck. The trough is constructed out of marine-grade aluminium. (It took weeks of drawing curved templates on the studio floor to find the right curve in scale.) The wider end acts as a harbour for spot-lights and some African papyrus while the beds beside the water flow are clumped with stands of blue iris echoing the painting I'd admired indoors.

By a happy accident of dynamics, the water falls into the lower pond in a neat liquid twist of 180 degrees. I couldn't resist putting in an extra light to draw attention to this wonderful mini-drama. Low-voltage halogen lights draw attention to the walls and benches. Pebbles are graded from light to dark giving the riverbed more movement, and black bamboo grows down the northern border. The garden also includes a customised dog house for the canine members of the household built with the same timber as the deck.

The garden was quite difficult to engineer and construct so unfortunately the budget did not stretch to the elliptical table that was designed to match the curved channel, but a fine substitute was located. Two years on now, and though the novelty of a new garden has worn off, the owners are as entranced as ever with the results of our collaborative journey.

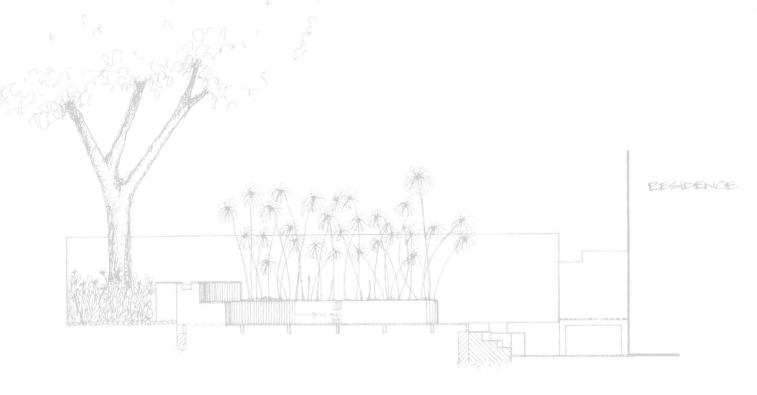

RESIDENCE

WHEN I LOOK AT THIS GARDEN I SEE ALL
THE BASIC ELEMENTS THAT ENCAPSULATE
MY DESIGN ETHIC: INCREMENTAL CHANGES OF
LEVEL, WATER-TRAILS CRADLING THE SEATING
AREA IN SINUOUS CURVES, SIMPLE UPRIGHT
STRUCTURAL FOLIAGE THAT MAXIMISES
SCREENING WHILE INCREASING USEABLE
FLOOR-SPACE AND FINALLY, A SUBTLE BLEND
OF NATURAL AND MAN-MADE MATERIALS.

DESIGN KEY

65 mm x 19 mm oiled ironbark decking

Walls are clad with 1800 mm-high Natureed in 3600 mm sheets.

12-volt, 50-watt step lights in the benches and retaining walls

Limewash Boncote, 'bark'

A marine-grade aluminium trough is set into the brickwork.

Black polished Chinese pebbles, 20-30 mm

'Anvil' granite pebbles, 50-75 mm

'Cowra' white pebbles, 20-30 mm

Plants

1 Sweet Flag *Acorus gramineus* 'Ogon'
2 Dutch Iris *Iris x xlphium*
3 Water Lily *Nymphaea* sp.
4 Black Bamboo *Phyllostachys nigra*

NOT PICTURED HERE
Umbrella Sedge *Cyperus involucratus*
Small Leafed Stretitzia *Strelitzia reginae* var. *parvifolia*
Papyrus *Cyperus papyrus*

SERENITY

The naturopath who owns this property wanted a garden that reflects the peace and tranquility she aspires to in her daily practice. There is a strong element of eastern spiritualism in her work, so we decided that a blend of influences emanating from this part of the world would determine the theme.

The rear doors of the house open out onto a wide timber deck which 'breaks up' into small pontoons that step down through the garden. At night this path is lit with strategically placed mounds of white quartz pebbles. Halogen lights deep in the core give the luminous milky stones a soft romantic glow.

Dominating one side was a large expanse of garden wall that was clearly ideal for a water feature. Long wooden channels set at different levels pass steady streams down the garden to the pond. At the time this was being drawn up I had just hired a new draftsman and I must give him full credit for the water emitters (sets of gracefully tapering slats) which we affectionately called the 'pagoda emission feature'. The base of the water wall has a safety feature with a difference: turpentine slats laid on edge form a wooden grill that makes it impossible for children to access. Water plants grow in between the slats and large granite pebbles are placed at random to break the flow.

For the main structural addition, my mate Trevor (a licensed carpenter and thatcher) built a Balinese pavilion over the deck with a traditional Alung-Alung thatched roof that catches the morning sun. A small raised deck around the outdoor spa on the western wall makes access easier and encourages people to congregate.

The garden is filled with port wine magnolia (*Michelia figo*), cycads, *Ajuga reptans*, *Acorus gramineus*, dwarf papyrus, rhapis palms and bromeliads. Inspired by a recent trip to Thailand and the vibrant silk fabrics I saw there, I painted the walls a deep purple hue to provide a lush background to the tropical foliage.

Carvings, statues and furnishings were selected in close consultation with the owner. They complement every aspect of the design and highlight the sense of harmony that the garden evokes.

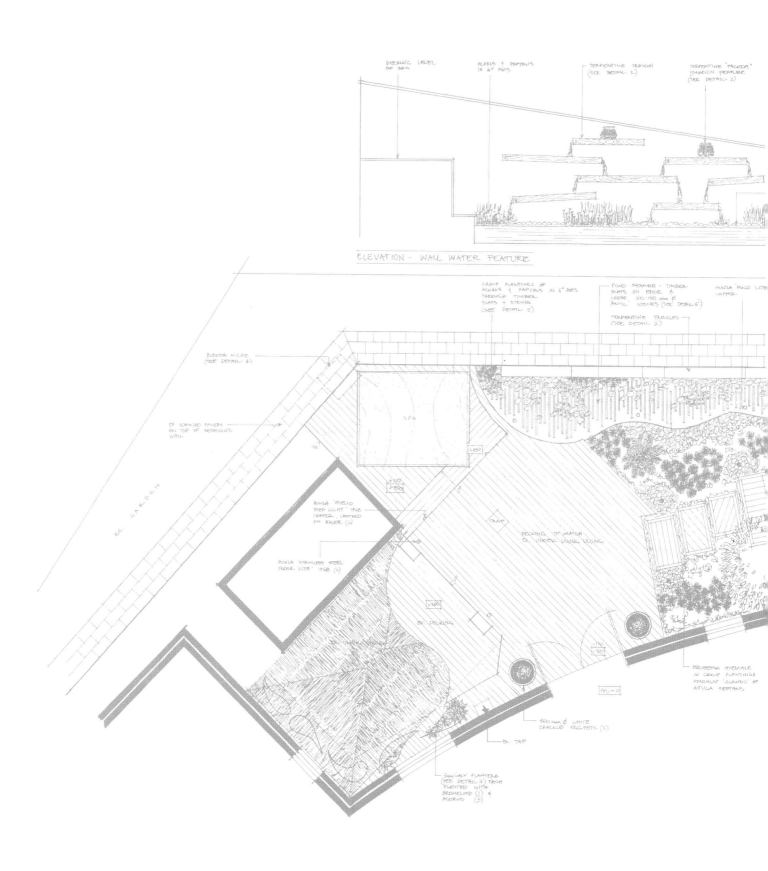

ELEVATION - WALL WATER FEATURE

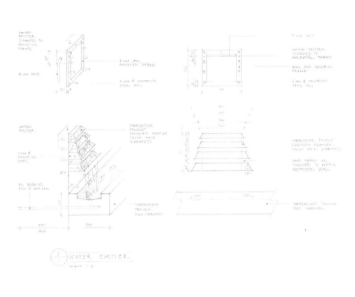

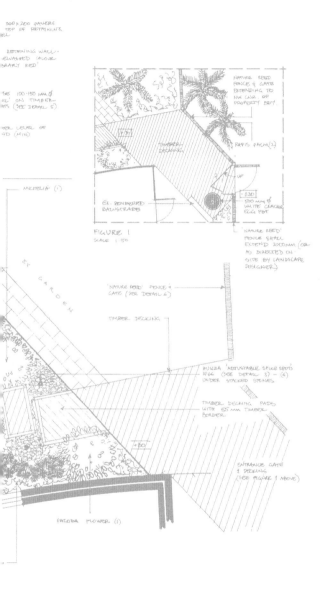

FIGURE 1
SCALE 1:50

WATER EMITTER

CARVINGS, STATUES AND FURNISHINGS WERE
SELECTED IN CLOSE CONSULTATION WITH THE
OWNER. THEY COMPLEMENT EVERY ASPECT
OF THE DESIGN AND HIGHLIGHT THE SENSE
OF HARMONY THAT THE GARDEN EVOKES.

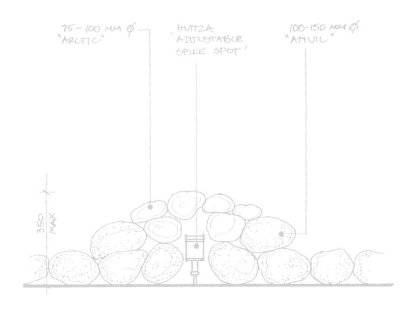

75–100 MM ∅ 'ARCTIC'

HVITZA 'ADJUSTABLE SPIKE SPOT'

100–150 MM ∅ 'ANVIL'

350 MAX

③ PATH LIGHTING

DESIGN KEY

Limewash Boncote 'iris' has a double-strength base to keep the colour rich and deep.

'A1' quartz gravel, 2-3 mm

'Artic' quartz pebbles, 75–100 mm and 100–150 mm

Decking and pontoons are constructed from 90 mm x 19 mm tallow wood.

'Anvil' granite pebbles, 50–75 mm.

Tilted Turpentine troughs with 'pagoda'-style emitter

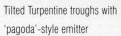

12-volt, 50-watt spike spot-lights are set inside piles of pebbles.

Plants

1 Lady Palm *Rhapis excelsa*
2 Yucca *Yucca elephantipes*
3 Cycad *Cycas revoluta*
4 Carpet Bugle Weed *Ajuga reptans*
5 Sweet Flag *Acorus gramineus* 'Ogon'
6 Umbrella Sedge *Cyperus alternifolius*

NOT PICTURED HERE
Bamboo Palm *Chamaedorea erumpens*
Clivea *Clivia miniata*
Port Wine Magnolia *Michelia figo*
Brush Cherry *Syzygium paniculatum*
Dwarf Papyrus *Cyperus papyrus* (dwarf)

GARDEN CASCADE

On a scale of one to 10, this internal garden was 9.99 in terms of difficulty. The house is a renovated terrace with an open-roofed internal courtyard that could be viewed from all three storeys. It has a very small ground area so quite a lot of the features we brought in were designed to be fixed to the walls. A pale colour scheme to brighten and expand the space was the obvious choice and you can't get much lighter (or more elegant) than white on white.

First thing was to explore the living spaces, taking photographs from every window and establishing the function and primary occupant of each room. Windows should always be treated as a critical viewpoint. If the room is a study, someone could well be spending several hours a day gazing through the glass so it's important to set up each view as an exclusive picture in itself.

A glass wall adjacent to the open stairwell sections off the garden from the house. The family of four had lived in Asia for some years so with this influence in mind I found some Balinese bowls with hand-carved frangipanis clustered around the rim. These were cut in half, remoulded, filled with

Spathiphyllum and fixed at intervals up the wall.

At ground level, a large stone trough catches the spill of three Balinese water spouts carved in a lotus shape. These are fixed in a panel of small travetine marble tiles laid on the diagonal which act as a splashback for the trough. Balinese green stones form a border for the tiles and are in turn framed by a moulded concrete architrave with creeping fig clinging to the walls on either side. White-glazed hibachi bowls holding two majestic andhurium sit on matching pedestals that flank the water feature.

A timber trough along the glass wall contains a row of black voodoo bromeliads and another trough holds giant mondo that runs around the base of the pond.

A larger version of the marble tile covers the floor and the same Balinese green stone forms a mosaic feature between the tiles.

This predominantly vertical 'canvas' is a combination of careful planning and meticulous placement which succeeds in making every room feel as if it has its own personal garden-scape.

LEVELS OF BLUE

Though this small garden belonging to an apartment-style house had the advantage of being split-level, it was just an unfenced patch of overgrown lawn when I first saw it. The owners are a young couple – he's an industrial engineer and she's a cellist – so I was immediately thinking of a space that was clever, private, intricate in detailing and generously proportioned.

I'd recently learnt about a quarry on the outskirts of Canberra that supplied a dark, dense split-face bluestone that I was dying to use. It would be perfect here but we nearly had to scrap the idea when the quarry became snowed in. Sighs of relief all round when a delivery finally arrived with a load of superbly mottled shards of stone.

The sunken area at the foot of the garden was ideal to promote as an area to congregate, barbecue or just relax in the sun, but there was a problem of privacy. A series of horizontal timber slats form louvres to raise the rear wall of the garden. They not only enclose the space but also screen the upstairs balcony from the neighbours at the back. More louvres like this separate the two levels of the garden and give the lower courtyard an intimate closed-in feeling.

The water feature came from an idea I'd been nurturing for several months after flicking through photos taken on a trip to England years ago. Beautifully preserved stonework characterises the historical city of Bath, and it conjured an image of thick stone tablets with clean, precise lines and water streaming across the surfaces. Following this idea, the slabs are fixed in an L-shape with sharp perpendicular angles bringing to mind a strong but simple Japanese form.

The remaining bluestone slabs are positioned in angles around the rest of the garden and immersed in a sea of polished black pebbles. A row of sacred bamboo (*Nandina domestica*) borders the eastern side of the property, leading down to a Japanese cherry tree with deep crimson leaves that pick up the colour on the timber louvres. *Cordyline fruticosa* 'Rubrum' planted around the tree also echoes the rich colour above. For ease of access to all parts of the garden, a set of timber stairs links the upstairs balcony to the lower courtyard.

The standout factor here is the colour palette: rich earthy hues with ruby highlights all held together by the 'gift' of natural bluestone.

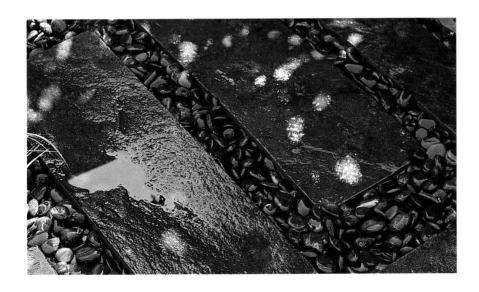

RICH EARTHY HUES WITH RUBY
HIGHLIGHTS ALL HELD TOGETHER BY
THE 'GIFT' OF NATURAL BLUESTONE

PURE AND SIMPLE

Japanese gardens are all about drawing upon the purest elements of nature: wood, stone, water and plant. Such inherent simplicity has inspired many of the world's best contemporary designers.

This garden expresses the fine art involved in Japanese gardens by combining both traditional and contemporary elements. The front entrance courtyard is set out according to the ancient principle of the wandering path. Instead of following a straight line to the door, the viewer winds through the garden and is encouraged to stop at strategic points to enjoy each feature for its own sake and for the way it relates to the garden in its entirety.

Bamboo is an intrinsic part of Japanese design. Most of us think of bamboo as a plant rather than a building material, but for thousands of years bamboo has been used in the East for the strength and versatility it offers in the construction of fences, bridges and even houses. Bamboo is one of my favourite plants for its versatility in colour, shape, height and texture. Here it is used for bench seating and pontoon stepping pads.

Crushed quartz and smooth river stones are carefully graded in an interpretation of the tradition of raked sand. The quartz was chosen for its reflective qualities, highlighting the vibrant hues of lush green plants and warm brown materials.

Banners of crimson silk ripple gently, accenting the red tips of blood grass, and the delicate Japanese maple (*Acer palmatum*, an essential part of any Eastern garden) proudly bearing its autumn display. The garden also features *Cycas revoluta*, an ancient slow-growing palm with beautiful architecture, *Imperata cylindrica* (Japanese blood grass) with its fabulous red leaf tips as a massed feature, *Acorus gramineus* 'Ogon' (great for borders) and *Liriope muscari,* which takes sun and shade and is very versatile.

Behind the bamboo bench, copper louvres are a distinctive feature with water flowing down the length of each shutter and illuminated by fibre-optic cables for night-time.

A powerful abstract stone sculpture by Melbourne artist Ashika beneath the branches of the Japanese maple stands in a river of large slate-grey pebbles. Enclosing the entire display are sheets of Natureed with several varieties of bamboo providing clouds and lines of subtle foliage.

DESIGN KEY

White 'A1' quartz angular gravel,
approx. 2–4 mm

Bamboo poles with a 50 mm
diameter are lashed together with
galvanised wire and screwed into
treated pine frame to make the
pontoons and bench seating.

A bamboo frame suspends 3000
mm x 450 mm drops of red
Japanese silk, decorated with
abstract ink drawings of iris.

The water stone is carved by
Ashika of Melbourne from basalt
with open-side coated with
lichen and moss.

Green 'hotham' pebbles,
30–50 mm

1800 mm x 3600 mm sheets
of Natureed cladding

The water feature's shutters
are made from copper.

Plants

1 Japanese Blood Grass *Imperata cylindrica*

2 Black Bamboo *Phyllostachys nigra*

3 Giant Buddha Belly Bamboo *Bambusa vulgaris* 'Wamin'

NOT PICTURED HERE

Japanese Maple *Acer palmatum*

Sweet Flag *Acorus gramineus* 'Ogon'

Blue Bamboo *Drepanostachyum falcatum*

Fernleaf Stripestem Bamboo *Bambus multiplex* 'Fernleaf Stripestem'

Pygmy Bamboo *Pleioblastus distichus*

Cycad *Cycas revoluta*

Lily Turf *Liriope muscari*

RUSTIC HUES

The arid beauty of the landscape, the stark naive architecture and the brilliant colours of Mexico ... this is the powerful combination I hoped to capture in this installation.

The garden is framed by a kind of forum, with large sleepers sunk into the ground like sentry posts and joined together with a lintel that continues around the perimeter. For a rustic finish, the beams are lime-washed and sandblasted so the raw grain of the timber stands out in sharp relief through the white. All the timber underwent this process, imbuing the garden with a sense of age and character.

Large bluestone slabs lie at the entrance. They are all cut to the same length but the width of each diminishes as the slabs approach the door – this is a useful trick to give the illusion that the path is longer than it actually is. The mirage is accentuated when gravel or a groundcover fills the intervals and in this case crushed lime glass is a vivid contrast to the bluestone.

The pathway edges are blurred with a mossy groundcover called *Scleranthus biflorus* which also surrounds two ramped garden beds filled with golden barrel cacti. An L-shaped timber seating area dominates the northern side of the garden and, directly opposite, the furry white tips of a grove of cat's tail cacti catch the morning sun. Nearby, a collection of agaves in terracotta pots stand at varying heights on timber pedestals. On the west side a tall upright garden bed filled with euphorbia contains two timber water features where a small fountain gushes from the tips of each post.

A selection of succulent groundcovers in grid form fill the foreground of the garden, with black roses and kalanchoe standing out in elevated mounds. Crushed charcoal slate surrounds the bluestone steppers and the recessed panels of the timber bench seating are painted an intense purple tone.

CIRCLE IN THE SQUARE

The arts and crafts of Turkey have had a powerful and enduring influence on interior design – and I don't just mean carpets. Traditional colours, textures and shapes were the inspiration behind this small interior courtyard open to the sky that I modelled on a simple village dwelling. A very talented importer agreed to lend some of her exquisite antiques to the display. She surely has the greatest collection of Turkish wares in Australia and we took full advantage of her generosity.

Water pours from an antique marble basin at the back of the main centrepiece, creating a transparent liquid curtain in front of a mosaic of tiles. The beautiful swirling pattern on these ceramic pieces features a traditional floral design that can still be admired today on the walls of historic buildings in Istanbul. Either side of the basin a shelved masonry altar displays graceful urns glazed deep green and blue against a lime-washed turquoise wall. The colour theme continues with lime-green glass mosaic tiles lining the central pond.

Squatting in the pond is one of the most beautiful urns I have ever seen. Recently unearthed from an ancient Turkish city, this ancient clay vessel is almost 60 mm thick in some places. It also took six men to lift. A fountain bubbles away merrily in the centre of the urn and tall and short varieties of papyrus soften the hard scrape of the pottery.

Two rusty old iron window grills decorate the panels on either side of the garden and terrazzo pavers flecked with green glass are cool and soothing underfoot. Small white timber pergolas were erected to support two antique butter churns suspended on ropes so their shapes can be fully appreciated.

Brass lanterns cast a cosy glow at night and citrus trees fill the air with their tangy scent.

PLANT
WISH-LIST

IF SOMEWHERE IN THE WORLD THERE IS A GARDEN THAT CATERS FOR CLIMATES FROM TEMPERATE TO TROPICAL, THESE ARE THE PLANTS I WOULD FILL IT WITH. DREAM ON...

SILVER TORCH CACTUS
Cleistocactus strausii
Covered in fine white hairs, this cactus looks incredible in front of a bold-coloured wall. Its erect form provides texture and structure and the pale aura of hairs looks glorious in the sun or uplit at night. Cats Tails need extremely well-drained soil in full sun and they love a well-ventilated position.

GOLDEN BARREL CACTUS
Echinocactus grusonii
These guys are a fantastic focal point for an arid-style garden and look great en masse if you have the budget for it. They like full sun, well-drained soils and I recommend a bold-coloured stone mulch to make them look their best.

ZERA GRASS, VARIEGATED EULALIA
Miscanthus sinensis 'Zebrinus'
Probably one of the least invasive ornamental grasses around, its distinctive stripy leaves are a perfect foil for plants with strong architectural form. This grass loves full sun in a well-ventilated position and under the right conditions can grow up to three and a half metres in height.

WATER LILY
Nymphaea cvs
An ideal plant to complement any water feature (especially ponds), it will die back in the winter but burst forth in full flower when the weather warms up. I find they grow best when submerged in their pots just below the surface in a warm, sunny spot.

ELEPHANT'S EARS, TARO
Colocasia sp.
A majestic tropical plant with generous tapering leaves that make the garden look lush and bountiful. It likes to be well-mulched in moist fertile soil and can take a full sun to semi-shaded position.

BLOODLEAF OR BEEFSTEAK PLANT
Iresine herbstii
This vibrant shrub can reach a height of 600 mm and its leaves can spread just as wide. Planted en masse, it creates a wall of colour that provides a striking visual contrast alongside grey foliage plants. It likes a warm, frost-free area and full sun.

FLOWERING BANANA
Musa ornata
Suited to warm tropical zones, this flowering banana is a superb accent plant. Its crimson stems can stretch to three metres in height.

LAMB'S EARS
Stachys byzantina
Soft and velvety like their namesake, the leaves on this silvery groundcover provide an ideal background for feature plants and prefer full sun and good drainage.

CARDBOARD PALM
Zamia furfuracea
A member of the cycad family, this tropical accent plant has strong linear branches radiating from a central trunk. They look wonderful when uplit and need to be kept well mulched in tropical zones.

AGAVE
Agave attenuata
Easy to spot with their thick spears of grey-green foliage, agaves combine a tropical but sculptured look and are particularly good for exposed, difficult sites.

PRIDE OF MADEIRA
Echium sp.
Recognisable by its great towering spires, the Echium has grey-green, sword-shaped foliage and purply-blue flowers. It prefers a cool climate with good drainage and lots of sun.

NEW ZEALAND FLAX
Phormium tenax
This New Zealand native has tall strappy leaves, is very hardy once established and comes in dwarf forms, too. The different varieties of foliage – from coffee-brown to burgundy to a white-variegated stripe - are great for experimenting with colour in your garden.

NEW ZEALAND CABBAGE TREE
Cordyline australis
Another gem from New Zealand, this small tree with rosettes of strappy leaves is a great accent plant with a uniquely eye-catching structure.

MAGNOLIA
Magnolia sp.
Although the magnolia is deciduous, it has a beautiful form whether in leaf, in flower or completely bare. Its large, fragrant flowers appear late winter through to spring and dwarf cultivars mean there is now a magnolia for all sized gardens. The evergreen variety is equally rewarding, with lemon-scented flowers for most of the year.

CHILEAN JASMINE
Mandevilla sp. *Sanderi* and cvs
Hailing from Central and South America, this hardy climber has showy trumpet-shaped flowers ranging from hot pink through pale pink to white. Evergreen in warm areas, it will grow huge with the right conditions and plenty of soil and if it's given a structure to twine onto, it will flower all winter long.

FRANGIPANI
Plumeria rubra
With its compact root system, this little tree is just as happy growing in a pot as it is in the ground. Its blossoms range in colour from white and yellow to deep gold and pink and they have a heady tropical scent. It needs well-drained soil and plenty of sun.

BIRD OF PARADISE
Strelitzia sp.
Another plant with a strong, sculptural form, the leaves vary from broad and almost banana-like to small and spoon-shaped. It withstands exposed conditions, likes sun or part shade and the exotic bird-like flower features brilliant streaks of orange and blue.

MADAGASCAR JASMINE
Stephanotis floribunda
An evergreen climber with glossy dark-green leaves and waxy pure-white flowers, it has a sweet subtle scent. Be sure to plant it in dappled light or the leaves will burn.

STAR JASMINE
Trachelospermum jasminoides 'Tri-colour'
If you are looking for something that provides a splash of colour all year around you can't go past this popular Jasmine with variegated new growth in pink and white. It's a vigorous climber but also very successful as a groundcover and fills an empty bed quickly.

BLACK LOCUST
Robinia pseudoacacia
I'm always looking for ways to use this lovely small shade-tree with a light feathery foliage that disappears in the winter months allowing the sunlight in. In multiples they do very well trained to a pleached form, where, side by side, they make an elegant elevated hedge.

PAPYRUS
Cyperus papyrus
Brilliant for adding an instant vertical element to a pond, this papyrus is a vigorous grower with long stems ending in bursts of fine green fireworks. The pot should be submerged just below water level and it needs lots of direct sunlight.

PURPLE CHERRY PLUM
Prunus cerasifera 'nigra'
Prunus looks wonderful showered in blossoms but even when not in flower this tree offers abundant colour with its deep-purple, almost black leaves which glow ruby-red when the sun is behind them. Try it next to a Golden Robinia for glorious contrast or paint a background wall a dramatic colour to really show it off. Once established it's very hardy.

JAPANESE MAPLE
Acer palmatum 'Dissectum'
This compact little tree with an elegant weeping habit is a perfect feature in a confined space and is just the thing for a Japanese-influenced garden. When the nights turn cool in autumn the leaves turn to stunningly vivid shades and this is the ideal time to select your new tree based on the colour that best suits your garden.

CARPET BUGLEWEED
Ajuga reptans
Ajuga is a carpet-like ground cover with glossy green and purple, sometimes pink, leaves. Tough enough to take light foot traffic, it produces a spike of blue, pink or white flowers and thrives in part shade with plenty of moisture.

CORDYLINE
Cordyline fruticosa 'Rubra'
This tough plant with distinctive red and black leaves has been developed into several new cultivars with different leaf forms and plant shapes. It likes lots of sun but needs shelter from damaging winds to maintain fresh leaves.

BAMBOO

As you have probably noticed by looking at some of my work, I love bamboo. Over the years, bamboo has had a lot of bad press because of its wildly rampant-growing properties, but there are many wonderful non-invasive species, too. These clumping varieties of bamboo won't end up in your neighbours' backyard. There are also some great products on the market today like bamboo guard (a plastic barrier submersed into the soil to a depth of 600 mm surrounding the plant to stop invasive roots escaping). And there's always the option of contained planting: use it in areas that sit between masonry walls.

One of the fantastic things about bamboo is that it's a renewable resource that can be harvested every year, unlike our precious forests which can take hundreds of years to mature. Asia has been growing and harvesting bamboo for centuries, for anything from building products to food. The rest of the world is slowly learning about its wide range of uses and growing conditions in most of Australia are ideal. I am such a big fan I even bought a bamboo surfboard.

CASTILLONI BAMBOO
Phyllocstachys bambusoides
f. *Castilloni*

GIANT BUDDHA BELLY BAMBOO
Bambusa vulgaris 'Wamin'

TEMPLE BAMBOO
Sinobambusa tootsik

BLACK BAMBOO
Phyllostachys nigra

CACTUS

Next to bamboo, my other great plant obsession is cacti. Over the years I've built up a large personal collection of cacti and succulents and I can't resist including a couple of pictures of my 'babies' here. I love the *Aloe plicatilus* (below left) for its flat, finger-shaped leaves, and my rare giant-sized golden barrel cactus twins are truly my pride and joy (below right). The only problem is finding the perfect space to do them justice so it's fortunate that many of them can survive for months at a time out of the ground: I guess I just haven't found the right spot yet for this *Oreocereus* (opposite page).

Recently, I had the chance to show off some of my best specimens in all their glory in an exhibition garden. The organisers were crazy enough to give me a massive budget and no brief. Dangerous, huh? Some of the golden barrel cacti are nearly 60 years old, worth up to $7000, and are so big (nearly a metre wide) they had to be fork-lifted in. It was a super-human effort from all involved, but the results were worth it.

Here's the plant list for all you wannabe collectors and cacti-philes:

Aeonium arboreum 'Zwartkop'

Agave americana var.

Agave attenuata

Aloe ferox x arborescens

Aloe plicatilis

Beaucarnia recurvata

Bromeliad spp.

Carpobrotus acinaciformis

Cleistocactus jujuyensis

Cotyledon macrantha

Cotyledon orbiculata

Crassula perforata

Echeveria imbricata

Echeveria violescens

Echeveria 'Violet Queen'

Echinocactus grusonii

Euphorbia trigona

Sedum morganianum

Sedum rubrotinctum

Senecio serpens

Stenocereus

Tillandsia usneoides

Tricocereus pachanoi

Tricocereus spachianus

Yucca elephantipes

Acknowledgements

There are so many people I need to thank both professionally and personally that it's hard to know where to start so please forgive me if I happen to miss anyone.

Putting a book like this together has been a dream of mine for many years, and I can't tell you how satisfying it is to see my work presented so beautifully. First and foremost, thank you to Sue Hines and Richard Walsh for believing in the project and teaching me how to make good books. Although I'm still a novice, I can't wait to do another! To Jennifer Castles and of course Rachel Lawson at Allen & Unwin, thank you for helping my 'gibberish' make sense. To Nick Mau, thank you for laying out the pages with such style and for making every shot feel as important as the next. To the rest of the great team at Allen & Unwin, thank you for making it all such a pleasure. And to David Matheson for your beautiful photography, your fantastic eye, your professionalism and patience.

Thank you to all of the wonderful lecturers at Ryde Horticultural College, in particular Tony Wilson for walking me through my first design. To Janet Bates for teaching me to stick photos of plants to my fridge so I could remember their names, and thank you also for your friendship and laughs. To Judy Fakes for teaching me that dirt is really 'gorgeous soil'. To Graham Fletcher for laying down the law about business and design, and for making it interesting and fun. And to my classmates, thank you for your friendship and support back then, even though half of you are now working with me – surely you didn't think it was going to end there did you? C'mon guys we're just getting warmed up!

Thank you to Helen, Michael and Karen for keeping the shop alive and beautiful while I was still finding my feet. To Don Burke, for your guidance and for believing in me and to all at Burke's Backyard magazine and CTC Productions, thank you for your smiles and support. To David Gyngell, Michael Healey, Mick Morris, Andrea Keir and the gang at the Nine Network, thank you for your support – you really are still the one! To Brian Walsh, thank you for your persistance in finally getting my dial on the tube and you're right, TV can be fun!

To my incredible management team of Chris Giannopoulos, Sean Anderson, Greg Hooton and everyone at IMG, thank you for your professionalism and constant support, I certainly couldn't

have done it without you. To Dolores and everyone at DLM, thanks for keeping it all together, and to Hanimax Fuji and Photo-Technica for your generous assistance.

To those who have inspired me over the years: Ricardo Legoretta, Andy Goldsworthy, Geoffrey Bawa, Frank Gehry, Frank Lloyd-Wright, and of course Paul Bangay, for your friendship and guidance.

And on a personal note, thank you to Nadine Bush for being there for me all the way, for your innate sense of style, for believing in me, and of course for your love and friendship. You are a talent and a true artist. To my mum thank you for teaching me the joy of gardening (pardon the pun: her name is Joy!). To Mum and Dad, thank you for supporting me and my career in whatever road it has taken over the years. I love you both. To my brother Chris, for keeping me in check. To Michelle and my beautiful Taylor and the rest of my family, thank you for putting up with my hectic life and for loving me all the same. Thank you to Chris Routledge, Tommy Cyr and James Houston for your undying loyalty and friendship and to the rest of my amazing friends: Charlie and Eve, Georgie and Johnny, Ian, Phil and Flick, Steve, Andy and Tracey and my housemate and buddy Tarquin – thanks for all your understanding, particularly when life gets a little crazy. (And Tarquin, sorry about the mess, I promise I'll do the dishes and put out the garbage next week!) To Colin Sainty for your friendship and for teaching me how to win medals. To Geoff at Arizona Cacti Nursery for looking after my 'babies' and to Mitch Bailey for teaching me the rules of the game. And to my beloved Blitz team: Scotty, Nig, Jode, Vid, Becky, Deano, Andy, Steve, Nicko, Neil, Brento and of course Rick Spence, for your friendship, laughs and guidance. Thank you also to the millions of viewers who tune in each week – without you guys the show wouldn't go on. Thanks too to Amanda Anderson (p.72), and all my wonderful clients.

And last but not least, boundless gratitude to my Patio family, past and present: Harriette, Chuck, Daniel, Geoffrey, Linda, Monica and Seb – thanks for putting up with my wacky ways. I hope you're all as proud of this book as I am. It's a testimony to all of your skills and hard work and none of it would have happened without you.

The Patio team: Harriette Rowe, a fourth-generation architect who after completing her degree decided to get a diploma in landscape design (she also helps organise my life which is another diploma altogether). Richard (Chuck) Berry, a landscape architect whose work is raw, uncompromising and often left-of-field, is an integral part of the Patio team. Sebastian Tesoriero, an ex-government lawyer who switched to landscape design, and whose phenomenal plant knowledge and legal savvy make him a handy guy to have around. Monica Levy, an interior designer who just happens to be a marketing whiz, has whipped our office into shape and put Patio on the map. And Linda Cox, a horticulturist/landscape designer with exceptional drawing-board skills who, luckily, can type faster than I can talk.

Thanks to the Royal Botanic Gardens Sydney for assistance.

ROYAL BOTANIC GARDENS SYDNEY

Note: All paints described in the design keys are Porter's.